MEL BAY PRESENTS

THE FLAMENCO/ CLASSICAL GUITAR TRADITION

VOLUME 1:

A TECHNICAL GUITAR METHOD AND INTRODUCTION TO MUSIC

BY JUAN SERRANO AND COREY WHITEHEAD

FREE An audio recording of the tracks in this book is available for download at:
www.melbay.com/21029

2 3 4 5 6 7 8 9 0

Visit us on the Web at www.melbay.com — E-mail us at email@melbay.com

TABLE OF CONTENTS

A Note from the Authors 8

The Guitar—A Brief History 9

La Guitarra (poem) 11

Preface 12

Parts of the Classical Guitar 13

Parts of the Flamenco Guitar 14

Names of the Open Strings 15

Tuning 16

Metronome 16

Note Locations on the Fretboard 17

Sitting Position and Holding the Guitar 18

The Fingers of the Right and Left Hand 22

Fingernail Shape and Maintenance 24

Picados (Scales) — *Apoyando* (Rest Stroke) and *Tirando* (Free Stroke) ... 26

Arpeggios (Broken Chords) 31

Tremolo (Preparatory Exercise) 35

Rasgueado (Strumming) 36

Basic Elements of Music Notation 41

Musical Expression Symbols 47

The Musical Alphabet 48

Half Steps and Whole Steps 48

The Major Scale 49

The Open Treble Strings 50

Systematic Arpeggio Exercises 53

Alternating Index and Middle Fingers 53

Sueño 54

The Open Bass Strings 55

Playing on the Bass and Treble Strings 56

Notes on the First String 61

Soleares 62

Notes on the Second String 64

Music in Two Parts 65

Playing Eighth Notes 67

Notes on the Third String 71

Sevillanas 71

Sevillanas I (Trio) 72

Sharps and Flats on the 1st, 2nd and 3rd strings 74

The Fifth Position on the First String 74

The Natural Sign 74

Romanza in A Minor 75

Romanza 76

Farrucas 77

Sixteenth Notes 78

Slurs 78

3

Estudio No.2 79

Estudio No.2 (Duet) 80

The Major Scale 82

The Natural (Relative) Minor Scale 83

The A Harmonic Minor Scale 84

The A Melodic Minor Scale 86

The Chromatic Scale 87

Notes on the Fourth String 88

Chords 88

Fandango 89

Fandango Duo 90

Notes on the Fifth String 91

Historia de un Amor 92

The Dotted Quarter Note 93

Perfidia 93

Notes on the Sixth String 94

Farrucas (Bass Line) 95

Farrucas 96

El Zorongo (Bass Line) 99

El Zorongo (Melody) 100

Playing the F Major Chord 101

Playing Two Notes Together (Double-Stops) 101

El Vito 101

Rasgueado 103

Sevillanas Intro 103

The Natural Notes 103

Sharps and Flats on the Bass Strings 104

The Chromatic Scale 104

El Rancho Grande 105

Alternating Bass and Chord Progression 105

El Rancho Grande (Duet) 105

Ascending and Descending Slurs: Ligados 107

Left Hand Agility Exercise 107

Chords in C Major and A minor 107

Las Mañanitas 108

Greensleeves 109

Scales and Chord Progressions 110

Rumba Rhythm 111

Scales and Chord Progressions cont. 111

The House of the Rising Sun 115

Variations on a Theme from Asturias 116

Malagueña 117

Intervals 120

Chords 122

Triads 122

C Major Arpeggio and Chord Inversion 123

The A Minor Arpeggio and Chord 123

The G Major Arpeggio and Chord 124

The F Major Triad 124

Barré Chords 125

Chord Progressions 126

Petenera 130

Café de Chinitas 131

La Virgen de la Macarena 132

The High D and E on the First String 133

Pica-Pica Melody (Guitar I) 133

Pica-Pica Accompaniment (Guitar II) 134

Pica-Pica Accompaniment (Guitar III) 135

Pica-Pica Accompaniment (Guitar IV) 136

Pica-Pica (quartet) 137

Key 141

Chord Substitution 141

Key Signatures 142

The Circle of Fifths 143

Major and Minor Scales in the First Position 144

More Chords in the Circle of Fifths… 160

Allegro by Ferdinand Carulli 161

Allegretto by Carulli 162

Andante by Carulli 163

Allegro in E minor by Carulli 165

Etude in G Major by Carulli 166

Andantino by Carulli 167

Larghetto by Carulli 168

Romanza 169

Menuet by Robert de Visée 170

Lección 38 by Dionisio Aguado 171

Clarines de los mosqueteros del rey de Francia by Sanz 172

Allegro by Mauro Guiliani 173

Andante by Ferdinand Carulli 174

Conclusion 175

About the Authors 175

Calle de las Flores, Córdoba, Spain
(Córdoba has been called the Birthplace of Flamenco)

Photo by Mark Langford

A NOTE FROM THE AUTHORS

Our goal in writing this book is to help the student in learning the basic technique and repertoire in both the flamenco and classical guitar traditions. We hope that this book gives you a better understanding of music and that it serves to improve your guitar technique. It would give us great satisfaction to know that this book has helped you in becoming a better guitarist. We hope that you carry on the rich tradition of the Spanish guitar and enjoy its music for many years to come.

Best Wishes,

Juan and Corey

THE GUITAR
A Brief History

The guitar is a descendant of two different instruments, the Spanish instrument called the *vihuela de mano*, and the European lute that descended from the Arabian *oud*. The Arabic word *oud* translates in English as "wood." The *oud* has six courses with the lowest sounding string being a single course. The word *course* refers to a single string or a pair of strings placed closely together. The European lute and the vihuela had a single high string or single course on top. On the lute this string was called the *chanterelle*. The vihuela and the European lute appeared in six-course versions. Various configurations of the lute used many tunings and had as many as thirteen courses.

The vihuela had as many as ten courses and was tuned like the modern guitar with the exception of the third string, which was lower by a half-step from the modern guitar tuning. It was tuned, from lowest to highest sounding course: E A D F♯ B E. The six-course lute was generally tuned, from lowest to highest: G C F A D G. There was no absolute tuning pitch at that time and some treatises instructed the student to tune the 1st string as high as possible without it breaking. The lute is often tuned a whole step higher to (A D G B E A) to take advantage of its more brilliant and shimmering tone quality at that pitch.

The earliest guitars date from around the middle of the 13th century in Spain and were mentioned in 1265 by Juan Gil of Zamora in the treatise called *Ars Musica*. In 1487 Johannes Tinctoris wrote about the four-course guitar being invented by the Catalans. The first music published for the four-course guitar was by Alonso Mudarra (1510-1580) in *Tres libros de música en cifras para vihuela* (1546). Nine books of tablature were published by Adrien Le Roy (1520-1598) between 1551-1555. These publications contain the first music for five-course guitar. Later in the same century Juan Bermudo (1510-15—) and Miguel Fuenllana (1525-1585) wrote music in tablature for the guitar. A treatise from the late 16th century in Spain refers to two techniques of playing the guitar; *rasgueado* (strumming) or *punteado* (picking with the fingers). The technique of alternate picking toward the palm of the right hand with two fingers, such as the index and middle fingers, was called *dos dedos*. There was a further explanation of a technique called *dedillo* that refers to a rapid up and down movement of the index finger to strike an individual string when playing scale passages.

The baroque guitar had five courses that were tuned to unison at the first, second, and third strings and to an octave at the fourth and fifth strings. The two exceptions are that sometimes the fifth string did not have the *bourdon* or lower octave string, and sometimes the first string was a single course like the *chanterelle* of the lute. The former would make the fifth string the highest sounding string on the instrument, many performers preferred the latter, and some performers employed both. The fifth string was the highest sounding string and the fourth was the lowest. On the modern guitar the fifth string is tuned an octave lower than the guitar of Gaspar Sanz. In 1674 in Italy, Francisco Corbetta (1620-1681) published *Guitarre Royale*, dedicated to King Luis XIV of France.

In 1596 in Italy there was a school of guitar playing called the *Alpha Beta School*. The primary scholars of the school were Juan Carlos y Amat and Palumbi. They developed a system of chord notation that was noted with letters to describe the chord to be played. They also used the terms "rasgueado" and "punteado" in their treatise.

Between 1770 and 1800, the six single-course guitar was commonplace and following this development composers such as Fernando Sor (1778-1839) Spain/France/England, Mauro Guiliani (1781-1829) Italy,

Dionisio Aguado (1784-1849) Spain, Napoleon Coste (1806-1883) France, Ferninand Carulli (1770-1841) Italy , Matteo Carcassi (1792-1853) Italy, Guilio Regondi (1822-1872) France, England, Luigi Legnani (1790-1877) Italy, Johan Kaspar Mertz (1806-1856) Austria, and others led the greatest development period in the creation of repertoire for the guitar.

In the second half of the 19th century, the guitar maker Manuel Torres developed a larger version of the instrument that is still slightly smaller than most classical guitars made today.

The late 19th century and early 20th century were important years for the development of Spanish guitar repertoire. Francisco Tárrega (1852-1909) and Miguel Llobet (1878-1938) were important performer/composers that inspired a generation of composers and guitarists including Andrés Segovia (1893-1987). Segovia's 1916 performance at the Anteneo in Madrid was considered to be one of the most important in history because before that recital, most people did not believe that the guitar had the volume and projection to be heard in such a large hall. Andrés Segovia is credited with many collaborations with important composers to expand the repertoire for the guitar in the 20th century, and he, like Tárrega and Llobet, made many transcriptions of works for keyboard, cello and violin. Composers such as Federico Moreno Torroba (1891-1982) Spain, Mario Castelnuovo-Tedesco (1895-1968) Italy, Joaquín Rodrigo (1901-1999) Spain, Joaquín Turina (1882-1949) Spain, and many others made important contributions to the guitar repertoire because of Segovia. Many composers began to consider the guitar a legitimate instrument that was suitable for the large concert hall. As a result, the body of guitar repertoire was expanded exponentially. Segovia introduced the guitar to universities and conservatories and consequently there are many such institutions that offer degree programs in guitar performance and repertoire.

Parallel to the history of the modern classical guitar, beginning in the 19th century in Spain a tradition called *flamenco* was born. This style was the culmination of traditions hundreds of years old from Persia and Arabia converging in the southern region of Spain called Andalucia. The flamenco guitar style was traditionally used to accompany singers and dancers in a *tablao flamenco*, a kind of private party where singers, dancers, guitarists, and percussionists — clapping hands (palmas) and snapping fingers, or rapping on tables with knuckles, palms and fingers — would perform for hours through the night into the early morning inspired by each other, spirits (*duende*), and wine.

Later the flamenco guitar became a solo instrument. The first solo flamenco recital was given in New York's Town Hall by Carlos Montoya (1903-1993) in 1948. After Montoya came Sabicas. Sabicas performed solo flamenco guitar recitals in the United States at first, and later around the world. In 1960 in Granada, Juan Serrano (b.1934–) performed the first solo flamenco guitar recital in Spain. Juan Serrano was also the first to establish a flamenco guitar program in a university at California State University, Fresno in 1983. Paco de Lucía, Manolo Sanlúcar and a whole new generation of flamenco guitarists followed Serrano, Sabicas and Montoya in the solo tradition. This tradition did not exclude them from ensemble collaboration, and the new generation of flamenco players have incorporated characteristics of musical styles from around the world including jazz, rumba, Arabian/Eastern popular music, and Latin popular music. In addition, many non-traditional flamenco instruments such as the *cajon* (a box-like percussion instrument with a snare attached), violin, cello, electric bass, flute, keyboard, harmonica, and many others are used in the modern flamenco ensemble.

La Guitarra

By Federico García Lorca

Empieza el llanto
de la guitarra.
Se rompen las copas
de la madrugada.
Empieza el llanto
de la guitarra.
Es inútil callarla.
Es imposible callarla.
Llora monótona
como llora el agua,
como llora el viento
sobre la nevada,
Es impossible
callarla.
Llora por cosas
lejanas.
Arena del Sur caliente
Que pide camelias blancas.
Llora flecha sin blanco,
la tarde sin mañana,
y el primer pájaro muerto
sobre la rama.
Oh guitarra!
Corazón malherido
por cinco espadas.

The Guitar

The lament
of the guitar begins.
The crystals of dawn
shatter.
The lament
of the guitar begins.
It is no use to silence it.
It is impossible to silence it.
It weeps on and on
like water weeps,
like the wind weeps
over the snow-capped mountains.
It is impossible
to silence it.
It bemoans
distant things.
Sands of the burning South
longing for white camelias.
An arrow without target weeps,
an afternoon without tomorrow,
and the first bird dead
on a branch.
Oh guitar!
Heart badly wounded
by five swords.

This poem is excerpted from *Poema del Cante Hondo* (Poems of the Profound Song) 1921. Profound or "deep" song is a style of soulful singing typical of flamenco.

PREFACE

Primary Objective

The primary objective of this book is to introduce the beginning guitar student, or any guitarist who has not yet learned to read music, to essential elements of music such as pitch, rhythm, staff notation, dynamics, articulation, interpretation, compositional form, scales, chords, triads, and composition via classical and flamenco guitar technique.

The Flamenco-Classical Tradition

Many Spanish classical works are *aflamencadas* (inspired by and stylized to sound like flamenco). Some composers who fall into that category are Isaac Albéniz (1860-1909), Manuel de Falla (1876-1946), Joaquín Turina (1882-1949), Miguel Llobet (1878-1938), Francisco Tárrega (1852-1909) and Joaquín Rodrigo (1901-1999). On the other hand, some flamenco *falsetas* (variations) are inspired by or quote classical music, so it is natural that when writing a method for the beginning guitarist, that technique and repertoire from both styles of playing should be demonstrated to the student.

Course Goals for the Aspiring Classical Guitarist

Learning classical and flamenco guitar technique and repertoire will develop a strong technique in *picados* (scales), arpeggios (broken chords) and rasgueados (strumming) and will give the student the tools that are necessary to successfully interpret and perform not only Spanish music, but music of any genre. The development of flexor muscles (inside of forearm) and extensor muscles (back of forearm) of flamenco guitarists is typically more balanced and stronger due to the practicing of rasgueado in addition to scales, *ligados* (slurs) and arpeggios. Although classical guitarists do use rasgueado as they become more advanced, generally, the extensor muscles are not developed from the beginning of a student's study of the classical guitar. This leaves some classical guitarists deficient in that area. One of the aims of this textbook is to remedy that problem.

Course Goals for the Aspiring Flamenco Guitarist

In studying this textbook, the beginning guitarist who only wants to play flamenco will not only acquire the basic tools for flamenco guitar performance, but also will acquire a technique that allows for greater tonal variety and promotes the ability to interpret polyphonic music in three and four voices simultaneously.

Goals

The student will understand and practice essential elements of music such as pitch, rhythm, sight reading, dynamics, articulation, interpretation, compositional form, scales, chords, triads, and composition via classical and flamenco guitar technique.

Upon completion of this book the student will have the technical tools, knowledge, and ability to learn and perform intermediate classical and flamenco repertoire and improvise chord progressions, melodic patterns, right-hand arpeggio patterns, and rasgueado patterns in all major and minor keys.

PARTS OF THE CLASSICAL GUITAR

Headstock

Tuning Machines

Nut

Fret

Neck and Fretboard

Heel

Upper Bout

Sound Hole

Rosette

Waist

Sides

Soundboard (Top)

Bridge

Saddle

Lower Bout

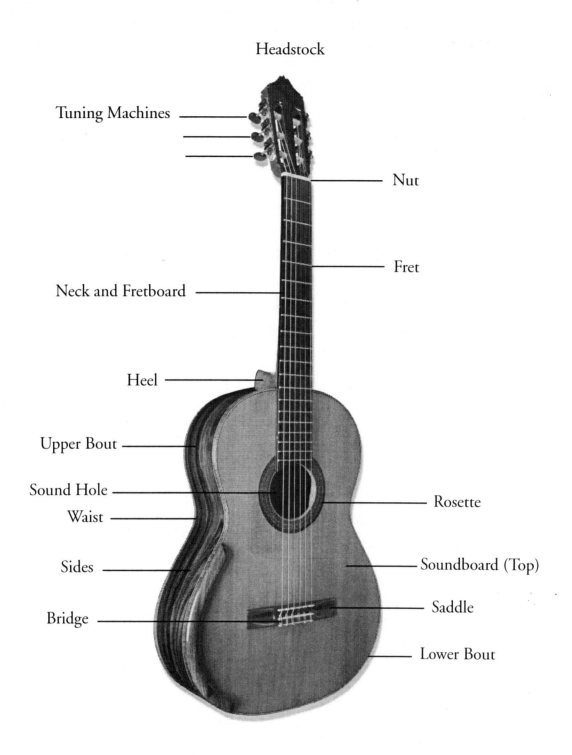

Guitar: David Schramm
Photo: Carlos de La Cruz with permission from Trilogy Guitars

Parts of the Flamenco Guitar

Tuning Machines
(Friction Pegs
on traditional models)

Cypress Sides (Blanca)

Golpeador (Clear Tap Plate)

Golpeador

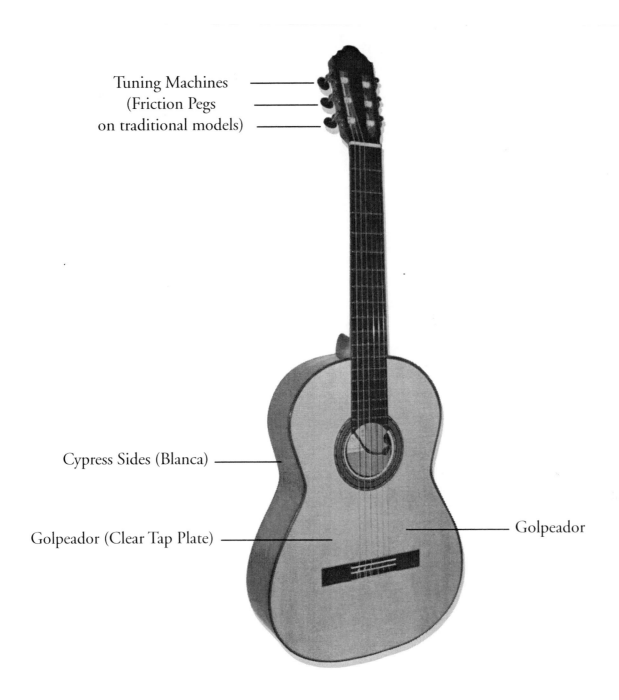

THE NAMES OF THE OPEN STRINGS

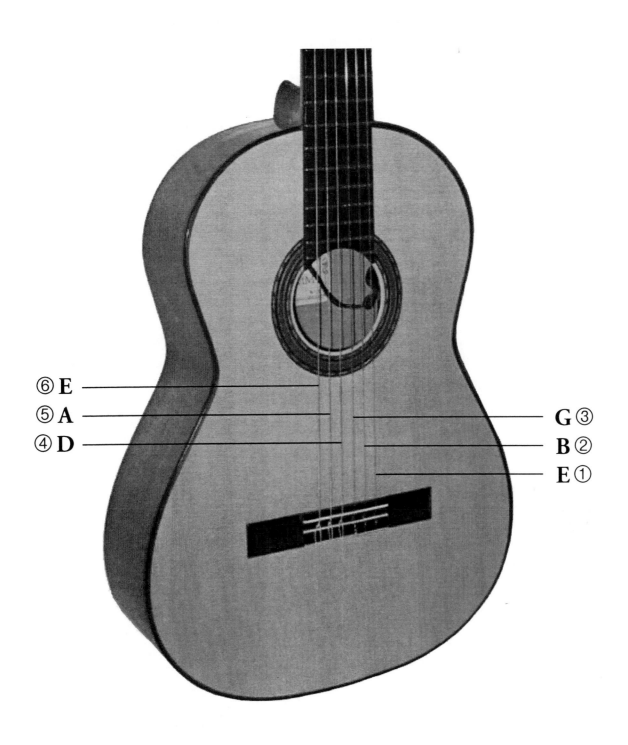

TUNING

For beginners particularly, we recommend using an electronic guitar tuner. A chromatic electronic guitar tuner can be purchased for between $20 and $100 U.S.D. depending on the model and features. All electronic tuners function in a similar manner. Play the open first string "E" and the tuner will display a letter name or a letter name and the sharp (♯) or flat (♭) symbol. The string should be adjusted by turning its corresponding peg or tuning machine at the headstock. When the peg is turned clockwise, the string is tightened and the pitch is raised higher according to the degree of adjustment made.

Turn the peg or machine counterclockwise to loosen the string and lower the pitch of the string. If the string is tuned too low in pitch, (which is usually the case with new strings because they loosen naturally as they stretch out) the tuner may show the "D" or "D♯" on the LED or display screen. Turn the machine or friction peg clockwise until the pitch reads "E" on the tuner. The needle that shows the fine tuning of the "E" should be directly on center where the two green lights appear and signal that the string is in tune. (Not all tuners have two green lights, so follow the instructions on your model). Repeat this process on the second string "B" and adjust the string higher in pitch until it reaches "B" on the tuner display screen. The second string may initially read "A" or "A♯" if it is tuned too low. The process should be repeated on the third string "G," the fourth string, "D," the fifth string "A," and the sixth string "E."

Note that on a traditional flamenco guitar the tuning pegs for strings 4-6 would have to be turned in the opposite direction than the treble strings to tighten them, i.e.-counter-clockwise, whereas tuning machines affecting all six strings of a classical guitar would be turned in the same direction to accomplish the desired effect.

METRONOME

A metronome is a device that produces a steady pulse or beat that can be set at any tempo between 40 and 208 beats per minute. A metronome helps to develop a steady internal clock or pulse that the musician can access when performing music at various speeds (*tempi*), even without having the metronome at hand. Sometimes a musician is required to play at various tempi within a single musical composition. While it is imperative to be able to keep a steady beat without the metronome, it is advisable to use a metronome when practicing any exercise in this book. Metronome markings are notated in the music with annotations such as "quarter-note = 60 bpm" (beats per minute). There is usually a further indication such as the Italian word *Largo* which translates in English to "very slow and steady." Other tempo indications will be explained later.

The metronome is usually adjusted with an analog dial, or up and down buttons that control a digital display screen. The number of beats per minute will be apparent on the screen and can be adjusted to the required tempo in the music. Usually, analog metronomes (with the dial adjustment) will have the Italian tempi markings for each tempo range. This is preferable and one brand that has such features with a volume adjustment is the Korg KDM-2 (Digital Clock Metronome with an analog dial). The KDM-2 also has an earphone jack and pulse light. There are many brands to choose from and they are constantly improving and becoming less expensive, so shop around before making your final choice.

NOTE LOCATIONS ON THE FRETBOARD

Basic Notes (A B C D E F G) and Sharps (A♯ C♯ D♯ F♯ G♯)

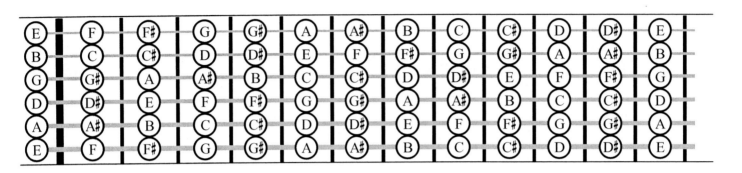

The notes that are placed on, below and above the musical staff represent pitches that are played on open strings or fingered on the fretboard at the locations shown above. The thick vertical line on the far left represents the nut. Each of the following vertical lines represents a fret. The fingers are pressed in the spaces immediately behind the frets. The faint horizontal lines represent the strings. The lowest sounding string is the lowest horizontal line (Low E, 6th string). The highest horizontal line is the high E (1st string). The pitch (note) names are placed on the horizontal lines that represent strings and between the vertical lines that represent their fret locations. For example, on the lowest line (Low E, 6th string) at the first fret, you will find the note named "F." On the third fret of the low E string you will find the note "G." Some fret and string locations may have two different note names, i.e. — the second fret on the sixth string may be called F♯ or G♭. The two names for the same pitch are called *enharmonics*. Sharps and flats will be explained in detail later.

Basic Notes and Flats (A♭ B♭ D♭ E♭ G♭)

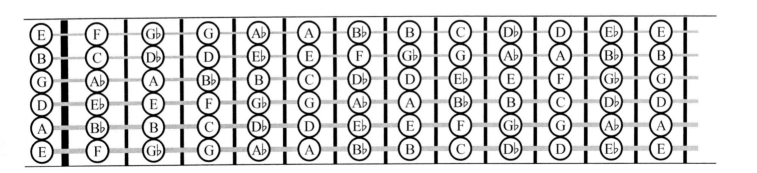

SITTING POSITION AND HOLDING THE GUITAR

Flamenco Sitting Position

The flamenco sitting position requires that both feet be placed flat on the floor. Occasionally, a footstool may be used for the right leg if the chair is too high. The lower bout of the guitar rests on the right leg and the right forearm rests on the lower bout, three centimeters or so behind the bridge. The guitar should be stable in this position without having to be held up by the left hand. The advantage of the flamenco sitting position is that because the footstool is not used, the performer has the ability to turn to either side to watch the dancers, as they move across the stage. The flamenco manner of holding the guitar also allows the performer to stand with the right leg elevated on a chair without changing the juxtaposition of the instrument to the player's hands and body.

Flamenco Right-Hand and Arm Position

The right forearm rests on the lower bout about three centimeters behind the bridge. Placing the thumb on the 6th string, flatten the hand so that the palm is touching all of the strings and the guitar top. Then, keeping the thumb in place, the index, middle and ring fingers are curved as if holding a ball until they are in playing position, whether on a single string for playing scales or on separate strings for an arpeggio.

Classical Sitting Position

In the classical sitting position the performer sits with the left leg raised on an adjustable footstool and the right leg placing its weight mostly on the ball of the foot as if you were about to stand up from your chair. The torso should be relaxed and upright, leaning slightly forward. The waist of the guitar may rest on the left leg or alternatively, the upper bout may rest on the left leg moving the guitar slightly toward the right. (This more closely assimilates the flamenco sitting position). The guitar should not be pressed flat against the body, but should lean back at angle toward the body, leaving a triangular gap between the back of the guitar and the torso. A very small part of the back of the guitar makes contact with the chest. The head should be balanced over the torso and not leaning forward in an attempt to see the fretboard. Rather, lean the guitar back toward the torso to view the fretboard.

Classical Right-Hand and Arm Position

To position the right hand for playing chords and arpeggios, place the right forearm on the lower bout just above the bridge and let the arm hang downward in a relaxed position. Then bend the elbow until the thumb is even with the 6th string. Place the thumb on the 6th string, making sure the thumbnail and flesh simultaneously make contact with the string. Relax the right-hand fingers and place the index finger on the 3rd string, the middle finger on the 2nd string, and the ring finger on the 1st string. Make sure the fingernail and flesh simultaneously make contact with the string.

THE FINGERS OF THE RIGHT AND LEFT HAND

Right Hand

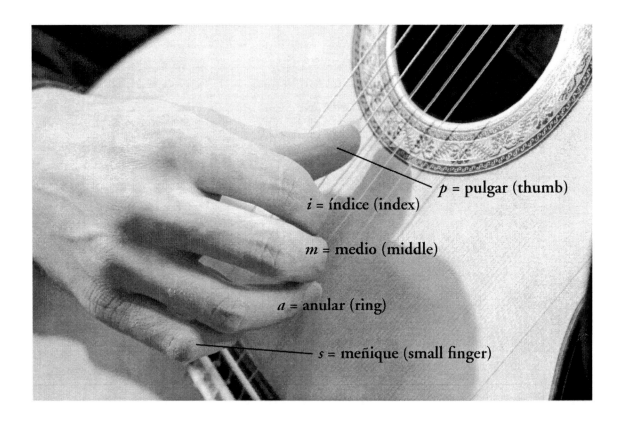

i = índice (index)

p = pulgar (thumb)

m = medio (middle)

a = anular (ring)

s = meñique (small finger)

Left Hand

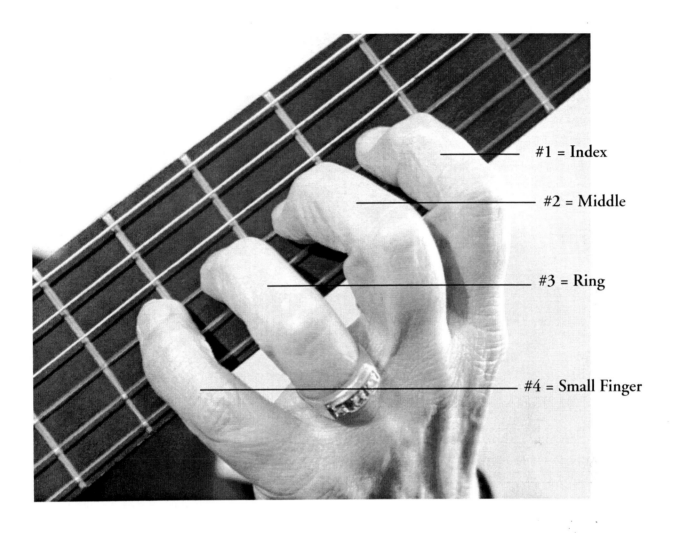

#1 = Index

#2 = Middle

#3 = Ring

#4 = Small Finger

Fingernail Shape and Maintenance

The fingernails of the left hand should be as short as possible so the fingers can press the strings to the fretboard directly on the tip of the finger on any string or fret. The fingernails of the right hand should be short where the flesh and fingernail meet on the thumb side, and slightly longer towards the little finger side. The fingernail should not make contact with the string before the flesh, otherwise a "click" will occur as the nail hits the string before the flesh. The click is eliminated when the flesh and fingernail make simultaneous contact. Every guitarist's hands are slightly different and individual preferences vary, so there is some room for variation in these "rules."

For example, the photo of Corey Whitehead's right hand on page 25 shows longer than usual fingernails. The fingernails are shorter on the side of the nail that is closest to the thumb and longer toward the outside of the hand. The file is held at an angle to the finger to create this shape. By contrast, Juan Serrano maintains a more rounded nail shape by holding the file directly perpendicular to the finger and filing squarely on the end of the fingernail. The sides are virtually left untouched, except for rounding and polishing the filed area to match the curvature of the fingernail. The little finger takes exception to all of this because for most players, it needs to be longer to more closely match the length of the ring finger when playing strums (*rasgueado*) with the back of the fingernails.

It is ideal to keep all fingernails at least 1/16" long, extending no more than 1/8" beyond the tip of your finger. The 1/16" length is preferable, but as fingernails wear and need to be polished or filed regularly they may become too short. Examine the fingernail length with the palm side of the hand facing you. Fingernails may appear longer in the view from the back of the hand because the nails may not attach to the flesh or the "quick" all the way to the tip of the finger. The "quick" may begin further down from the fingertip for some.

The fingernail may be shaped slightly different according to your basic nail and fingertip shape. Some players have fingernails that are well-suited for playing the guitar. Ideally, the nail is slightly rounded and strong, with no downward "dips" in the center (from a straight-on view directly at the fingertips), nor does it tilt upward at the center. They do not break or chip easily, or have any other defect, and they are easily kept in good condition. Usually, a rounded shape that follows the contour of the fingertip works well when filing fingernails of this type.

Many players are less fortunate in having fingernails that are not so well-suited for playing the guitar. If the fingernails are flat, they may wear down and eventually dip in the center. It is important to file smooth any spots that wear down and keep a smooth and consistent edge. This type of fingernail should be filed a little shorter on the side of the nail that is closest to the thumb, and a little longer toward the side away from the thumb. This shape allows the fingernail to pass over the string easily and will produce a warm, round tone. One excellent alternative to this fingernail shape is to change the angle of the file to the opposite direction. This makes the fingernail longer on the side closest to the thumb allowing it to cross the string very easily, and producing a similar tone from finger to finger.

The edges and underside of the fingernails should be carefully sanded and polished extremely well, almost as smooth as glass. The sandpaper of choice, 3M Tri-Mite 405N Wet-Dry sandpaper, is available from guitar string vendors on the Internet.

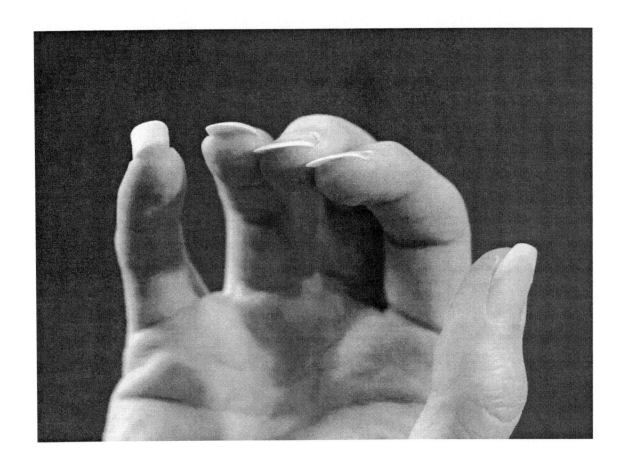

Any dips in the nail should be filed out from beneath the edge until it is flat. If your fingernails dip too severely, try using silk wrap nails from a nail salon or one of the various "players nail" products on the market, or ping-pong ball slivers affixed to the underside of the fingernail with Super Glue®. This works very well and can easily be done by purchasing a manicure kit with nail clippers, scissors, a diamond file, Krazy Glue® or Super Glue® (liquid, not gel), Prince Brand (Four Star) Ping-Pong Balls, and tweezers.

Ping-Pong Ball Nail Procedure

1) File the fingernail until there is 1/8" of nail left from the quick to the tip, this allows the fingernails to be filed short enough to be 1/16 to 1/8 of an inch beyond the tip of the finger.

2) Cut the ping-pong ball in half.

3) Cut a small semi-circle that fits comfortably under the nail and is in complete contact with the quick (where the flesh attaches to the fingernail).

4) Draw a line with a pencil indicating the outline of the sliver to be cut from the ball. Make sure that it is cut larger than needed to make a fingernail because the size will be reduced once it is glued under the real fingernail.

5) Cut the ball material along the pencil line.

6) Grab the sliver at the tip with tweezers and put a small bead of glue on the edge that goes under the fingernail.

7) Place the sliver underneath the nail, still holding it with the tweezers, and then squeeze the corners for about 10-20 seconds each; then work to the middle and all over until the glue is dry.

8) Use clippers, cut a straight edge on either side of the false fingernail parallel to the side of the actual nail.

9) Trim the tip of the false fingernail to the contour of the natural nail shape. File the underside, edge and top of the new fingernail.

10) Sand the nail with 3M Tri-Mite 405N Wet Dry sandpaper available from guitar string vendors online.

11) The ping-pong fingernail procedure leaves some glue under the fingernail on the flesh. Let it dry completely and it will peel off or come off easily with sandpaper or a file. Then it will feel more natural.

Ping-pong ball nails feel more natural after you get used to the shaping process, and let the glue completely fall off the flesh beneath the fingernail. They feel most natural after a day or two of playing, so don't put them on too close to a performance without having a great deal of experience with the process.

Picados (Scales) — Apoyando (Rest Stroke) and Tirando (Free Stroke)

Picados (scales) are the stepwise ascending or descending alphabetical arrangement of notes in music. They may be repeated (*tremolando*) or each note may only be played once, before changing to another note. The *apoyando* (rest stroke) is used primarily in playing scales and the *tirando* (free stroke) is used primarily in playing arpeggios (broken chords) and music in two or more parts.

The rest stroke is executed by pushing the finger toward the top of the guitar and momentarily making contact with the adjacent string before it relaxes and returns to playing position.

The free stroke is executed by pushing slightly in, toward the top with the right-hand finger, bending the middle joint of the finger and following through toward the palm of the hand, and passing over the adjacent string. Then the finger should relax and return to its ready position below the string just played.

The following scale exercises should be practiced with free stroke and rest stroke.

Ex. A — Prepare the thumb (*p*) and the index (*i*) where the nail and flesh make contact with the string simultaneously.

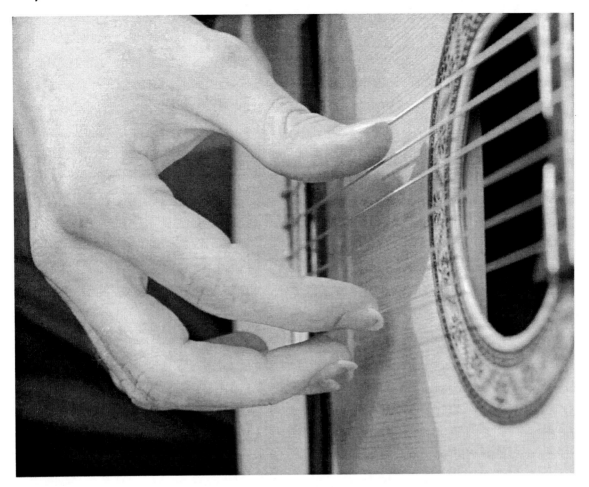

Performance notes for Rest Stroke

The right arm rests on the upper bout directly above the bridge, half way between the wrist and elbow. Rest the thumb on the 6th string, (Ex. A) The fingernail and flesh of the thumb simultaneously make contact with the string (fingernail shape and care is illustrated above). Now place the index finger on the first string in the same manner (with the fingernail and flesh of the thumb simultaneously making contact with the string). The thumb (*p*) is the anchor; it should not move. The index finger has been prepared, and is now ready to push in slightly toward the guitar top, following through until the flesh of the fingertip makes contact with the adjacent string (2nd string–B). The finger should immediately relax and return to playing position below the 1st string.

Ex. B — Press inward toward the top of the guitar with the large joint of the index (*i*) finger and follow through until the index finger momentarily comes into contact with the second string before relaxing and returning to its original playing position.

Next, prepare the middle finger (*m*) by placing the nail and flesh in simultaneous contact with the string. Then the "*m*" finger pushes the string slightly toward the soundboard of the guitar and makes contact with the adjacent 2nd string–B. It should immediately relax and return to playing position underneath the 1st string. Repeat this process on the 1st string and then do the same on the 2nd string; then move to the 3rd string and do the same. Repeat the process again on the 2nd string and the exercise is complete. Repeat the exercise for three minutes. Play with the metronome set to 60 beats per minute (bpm) playing once per beat. Play each finger combination at least four times rest stroke and four times free stroke.

Ex. C — Prepare the middle finger (*m*) on the first string

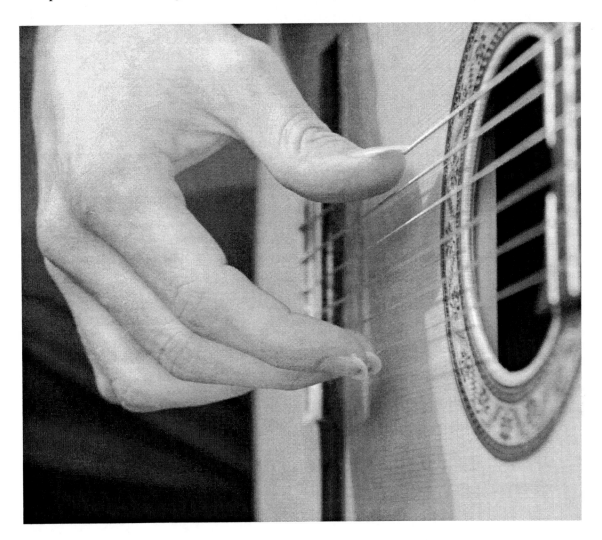

Ex. D — Press inward toward the top of the guitar with the large joint of the middle (*m*) finger and follow through until momentarily coming into contact with the second string before relaxing and returning to playing position.

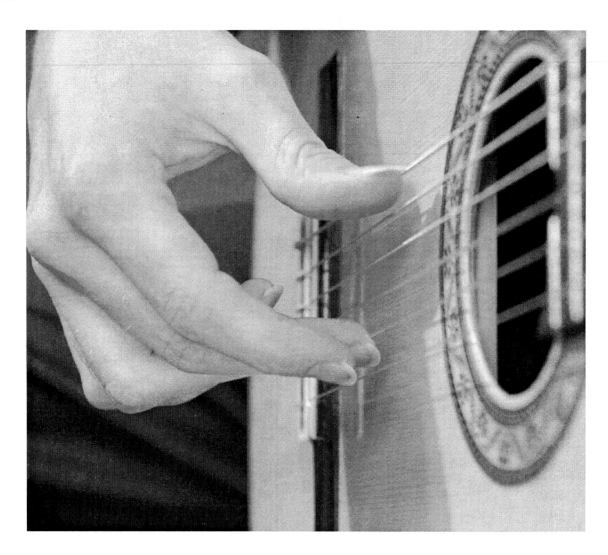

Finger Alternation Exercises

MAY 2013

100/200/250.260.270

Play each of the R.H. finger combinations in alternation on the treble strings as indicated by the numbers enclosed in a circle.

Ex: ① 1st string, ② 2nd string, ③ 3rd string, etc.

REST STROKE & FREE STROKE
4x   *6x*
DEC 2014   *60.70.80.90.100*

①———	②———	③———	②———	①———		
i m i m	*i m i m*	*i m i m*	*i m i m*	*i m i m*	*i* ———	*150.160.170.180*
mi m i	*mi m i*	*mi m i*	*mi m i*	*mi m i*	*m* ———	*190.200, 210.220*
a m a m	*a m a m*	*a m a m*	*a m a m*	*a m a m*	*a* ———	*230.240.250*
ma m a	*ma m a*	*ma m a*	*ma m a*	*ma m a*	*m* ———	*260.270*
i a i a	*i a i a*	*i a i a*	*i a i a*	*i a i a*	*i* ———	*280*
a i a i	*a i a i*	*a i a i*	*a i a i*	*a i a i*	*a* ———	
i m a m	*i m a m*	*i m a m*	*i m a m*	*i m a m*	*i* ———	

110.120.130.140

Try All @ 300 for Smoothness

240

Arpeggios (Broken Chords)

Right-hand preparation for playing an arpeggio

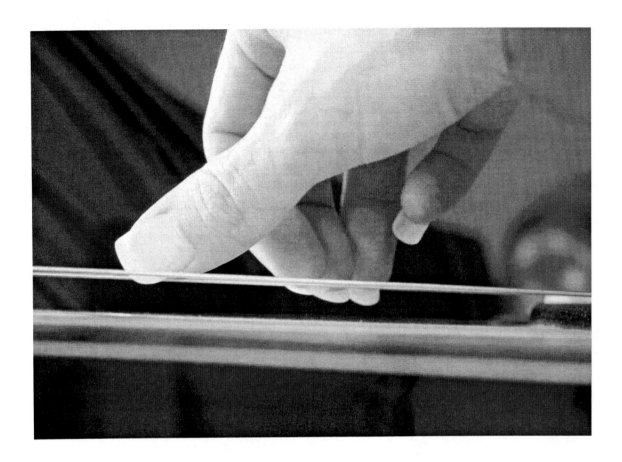

The flesh and fingernail simultaneously make contact with the string. Notice the thumb and index finger are perpendicular to one another. The thumb can reach slightly toward the soundhole and the fingers may slide slightly toward the bridge to assume this hand position. This hand position helps to prevent the thumb and fingers from making contact with one another.

Prepare the R.H. thumb (*p*) on the 6th string and the R.H. ring finger (*a*) on the 1st string.

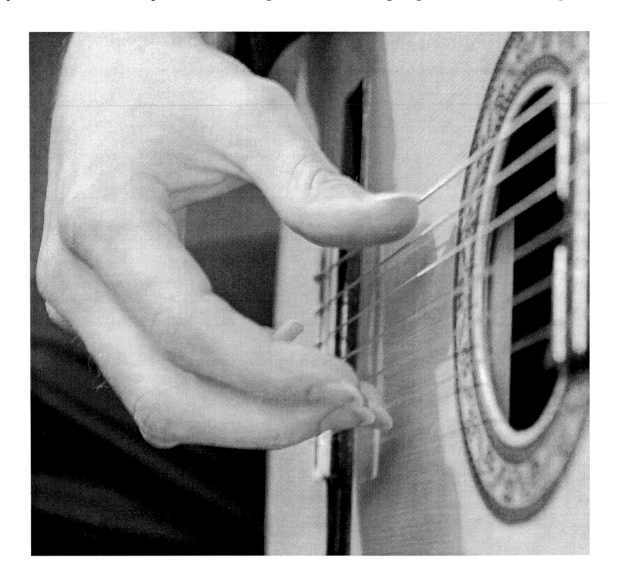

The right-hand thumb rests on the 6th string as described earlier and the *a* finger prepares on the 1st string with the fingernail and flesh of the thumb simultaneously making contact with the string. The *a* finger plays free stroke following through toward the palm by bending at the middle joint.

The *m* finger immediately prepares on the 2nd string (as quickly) as you can snap your fingers. Then play the *m* finger with a free stroke, bending at the middle joint, end following through towards the palm.

Immediately prepare the *i* finger on the 3rd string (as before) and then strike it, following through toward the palm.

The *m* finger extends outward to prepare on the 2nd string immediately and then plays toward the palm as the *a* finger extends outward from the palm to prepare on the 1st string to start the arpeggio again. Set the metronome to 60bpm and play one note per beat. Play each arpeggio eight times. Circled numbers represent the strings to be played;

ALL FREE STROKES

R.H. Arpeggio Exercises

Ex: ① 1st string, ② 2nd string, ③ 3rd string, etc.

①	②	③	②	①	②	③	②
a	*m*	*i*	*m*	*a*	*m*	*i*	*m*
②	③	②	①	②	③	②	①
m	*i*	*m*	*a*	*m*	*i*	*m*	*a*
③	②	①	②	③	②	①	②
i	*m*	*a*	*m*	*i*	*m*	*a*	*m*
②	①	②	③	②	①	②	③
m	*a*	*m*	*i*	*m*	*a*	*m*	*i*

MAY 2013

200 - Smoothness accuracy
↓
250 + speed
260
270

DEC 2014

60.70.80.90.100.110
120.130.140.150.160
170.180.190.200.210
220.230.240.250
260.270

280

34

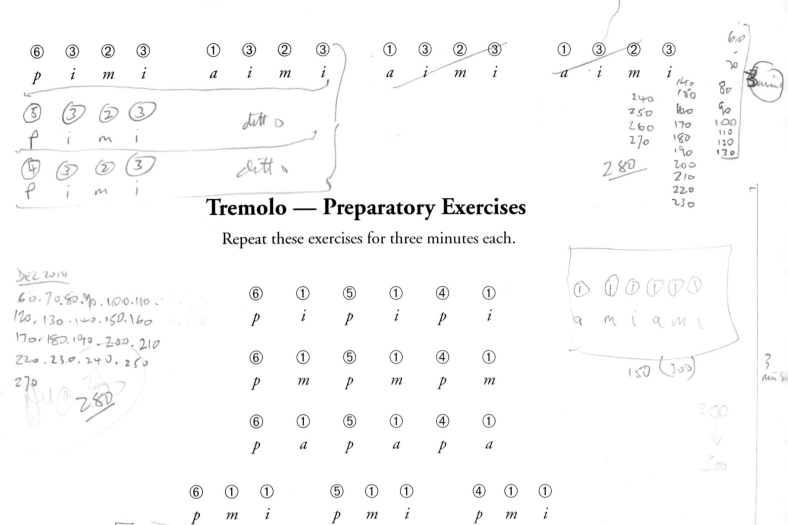

Tremolo — Preparatory Exercises

Repeat these exercises for three minutes each.

Thumb Exercise

Rest (*i, m, a*) on the treble strings; play rest strokes and free strokes:

four times each—— | two times each—— | and then once per string.

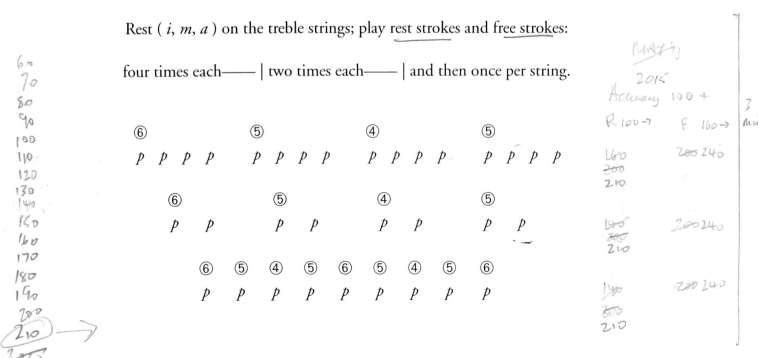

Rasgueado (Strumming)

There are two types of right-hand positions for *rasgueado*. The first is fixed with the right-hand thumb anchored on one of the bass strings. Rest the right-hand thumb on the 6th string. Close the hand with all fingers touching the palm.

Quickly strike the first three strings simultaneously with the back of the index fingernail.

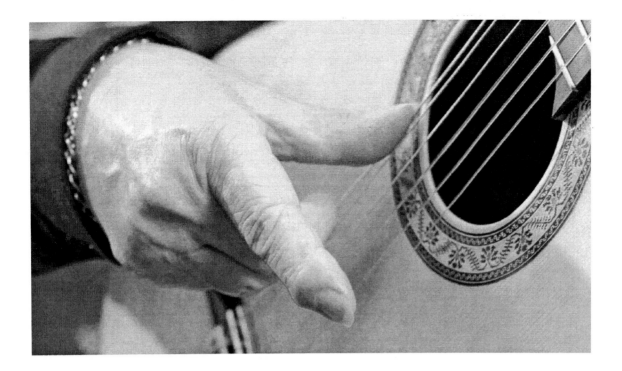

Then rapidly strike the treble strings with the back of the *s* finger and simultaneously bring the index finger back into the palm.

The *s* finger should remain extended. This is an important element in playing the rasgueado rapidly.

Next, strike the treble strings with the back of the a finger. Leave the *s* and *a* fingers extended.

Then strike the treble strings with the back of the middle finger. Leave the *m*, *a* and *s* fingers extended.

Then strike the strings with the *i* finger and simultaneously bring *s*, *a* and *m* into the palm in the ready position. This exchange of fingers is the second important element in playing a fast rasgueado. This movement of *i* restarts the rasgueado and should be followed by *s*, *a* and *m* as before.

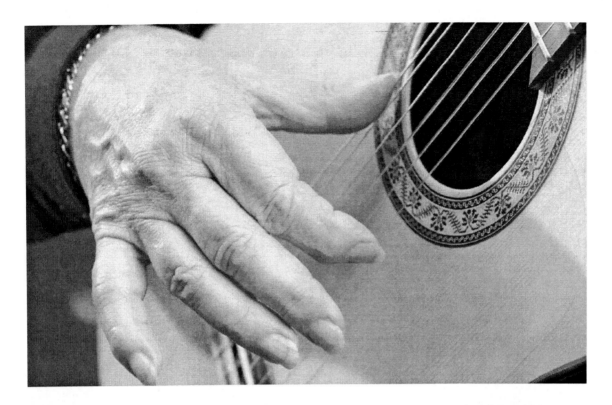

Set the metronome to 60bpm and play one finger stroke per beat. Practice at this speed for two minutes; increase the metronome speed by one notch once 60bpm feels comfortable and easy.

200 - warm up   MAY 13

240,   160   return ema to fist as

260   170   you play i

270   200

280   210

290   225

Other Rasgueado Patterns

Play each of the following patterns with down strokes while the thumb rests on the fourth string in fixed position. The back of the fingernail should quickly strike the 3rd, 2nd and 1st strings almost simultaneously. This motion of the right hand will develop the extensor muscles at the top of the forearm. These patterns should be practiced for an equal amount of time as the rest stroke and free stroke exercise shown earlier. Repeat each finger combination. Each stroke should be executed quickly and the beats should be of an equal duration. At first, the pulse should be set at about 60bpm on the metronome. Play one finger stroke per beat. When each pattern has been mastered at that tempo, increase the speed of the metronome by one notch. Accent the first strum of each two-strum pattern.

60
$$(i \ m) \ (m \ i) \ (i \ a) \ (a \ i) \ (a \ m) \ (m \ a)$$

The following patterns are played from the free right-hand position, that is, the thumb does not rest on one of the bass strings. The following patterns should be played with a down stroke by the *m* finger, followed by an upstroke by the *p* finger. Accent the first stroke of each pattern.

60
$$(m \ p) \ (p \ m)$$

The next pattern is a three-stroke sequence. Play from the free position and strike the treble strings (E, B, G) with an upstroke of the thumb. The second and third strums are played with consecutive down strokes on the treble strings. The right wrist should rotate slightly as if turning a doorknob.

60
$$(p \ a \ i) \ (p \ m \ i)$$

The next pattern is a four-stroke sequence. Play from the free position and strike the treble strings (E, B, G) with an upstroke of the thumb. The second, third, and fourth strums are played with consecutive down strokes. Again, the right wrist should rotate slightly as if turning a doorknob.

60
$$(p \ a \ m \ i)$$

BASIC ELEMENTS OF MUSIC NOTATION

Staff Notation

Staff notation is a system of placing symbols that represent pitches and their duration on a **musical staff** that has five lines and four spaces.

The bottom line is considered line number one and the top line is line number five. Likewise, the bottom space is number one, and the top space is number four.

Bar Lines and Measures

The staff is divided into measures by vertical bar lines.

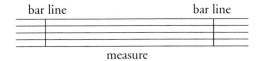

The Treble Clef

The **treble clef (G clef)** is used in guitar music notation. It is placed at the beginning of each line of music for the guitar. The treble clef sign consists of a single fluid line (see below) that passes through the second staff line four times. A note on the second line represents the pitch "G," giving rise to the term "G clef." The notes on the lines from lowest to highest are E-G-B-D-F (remember: **E**very **G**ood **B**oy **D**oes **F**ine) and the spaces from lowest to highest are F-A-C-E. (spelling the word **FACE**).

The Bass Clef

The **bass clef (F Clef)** is used for low-sounding instruments and voices. The note names of the lines are from lowest to highest: G, B, D, F, A (**G**ood **B**oys **D**o **F**ine **A**lways) and the note names of the spaces are: A, C, E, G (**A**ll **C**ows **E**at **G**rass).

The Grand Staff

The Grand Staff used to notate keyboard and harp music is the combination of a treble clef and a bass clef connected by a bracket. The ledger line note that falls between the staves is Middle C. On the piano, the notes that are played by the left hand are generally written in the bass clef and the right hand usually plays notes written in the treble clef.

Time and Meter

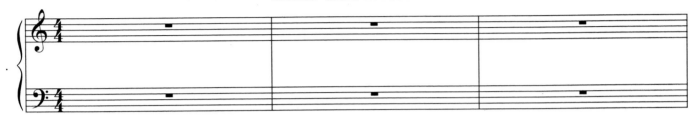

The terms "time" and "meter" are largely synonymous and refer to the grouping of beats and accents within a measure. The most common meter is **quadruple meter** (four beats per measure). Other commonly used meters are **triple meter** (three beats per measure) and **duple meter** (two beats per measure).

All of these are regarded as **simple meters**. In contrast, **compound meters** result from multiplying simple meters by 3; i.e. 2/4, 3/4, and 4/4 time would become 6/4 (compound duple), 9/4 (compound triple), and 12/4 (compound quadruple) respectively. These fractional symbols are explained below.

Time Signatures

Time signatures are designated by a fractional symbol at the beginning of a musical composition. A simple time signature indicates the number of beats per measure in the upper number, and the lower number indicates what kind of note is equivalent to one beat. Time signatures with an upper number of 6, 9, 12, or 15 are called "compound" time signatures or meters. The upper number of compound time signatures must be divided by three to determine the number of beats per measure. In modern music, it is also possible to encounter "irregular meters" or time signatures like 5/8, 5/4, 7/8, 7/4, 11/8 or 11/4.

4/4 or Common Time

In **4/4 time** the upper number tell the performer that there are four beats per measure and the lower number tells the performer that the quarter note is equivalent to one beat. This time signature is an example of **quadruple simple** meter. When the natural division of the beat is marked by the performer tapping his or her foot and/or counting, the beats may effectively be divided in two equal parts without a metronome. This is helpful when playing note values smaller than one beat each. The number is counted on the downbeat (the foot taps down on the floor) and the "and" is on the upbeat (with the foot in the air at its apex).

The subscript number 8 below the treble clef in the example below indicates that all notes are one octave lower than if written in the normal treble clef. This clef is sometimes used for guitar music, though a standard treble clef is more common, where the guitar actually sounds an octave lower than written.

Quarter Notes

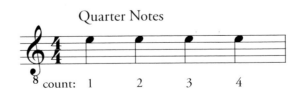

42

A stylized letter **C** is often used in place of **4/4** to indicate **common time**.

3/4 Time

In **3/4 time** (triple simple meter) there are three beats per measure and the quarter note is equivalent to one beat.

Music Notation Symbols — Duration of Notes

The notation of rhythm includes symbols that represent different note durations. In 4/4 time for example, whole notes sustain for four equal beats, half notes sustain for two equal beats, quarter notes ring for one beat, and eighth notes sustain for one-half beat. Notes have several different parts that distinguish them from each other:

Whole note
(open note head)

Half notes
(open note head with a stem attached)

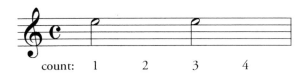

Quarter notes
(filled note head with stem attached)

Eighth Notes

The closed note head with stem attached to a flag or beam is called an eighth note. The beam is used to connect two or more eighth notes. (Single eighth notes have a flag in guitar music and will be illustrated later in the book.)

count: 1   &   2   &   3·   &   4   &

Playing Whole Notes

An open oval placed on a line or space represents a whole note. The note on the top space of the staff represents the open first string "E." Count four steady beats, or play along with the metronome before starting. Tap your right foot on each beat with the ball of the foot, leaving the heel on the floor. Lift the ball of the foot off the floor in between beats. The ball of the foot should reach its highest point at the midway point between the beats. The tap is the downbeat and the lift point between the beats where the foot is at its apex is the up beat. This is often counted:

	1	and	2	and	3	and	4	and
Right Foot:	tap	lift	tap	lift	tap	lift	tap	lift

Count and tap four beats before you begin. Then, play the open first string "E" on beat one and allow it to ring for four counts as you count and tap the remaining beats in the measure.

count: 1   2   3   4

Playing Half Notes

An open oval with a stem attached represents the half note. The stem is attached on the left side of the notehead if the stem direction is downward and on the right side if its direction is upward. If the note is above the third line, the stem should go downward. If the note is below the middle line, the stem should go upward. If the note falls on the middle line it may go upward or downward depending on the direction of most of the other stems in that measure. The half note sustains for two equal beats. Count four equal beats before playing the first note. Then play the open "E" first string on beat one and let it sustain through beat two. Then strike the open "E" again on beat three allowing it to sustain through beat four.

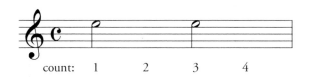

count: 1   2   3   4

Quarter Notes

A black note head with a stem attached represents a quarter note. Each quarter note has a duration of one beat. Therefore in the following example a note would be played on each beat of the measure.

Eighth Notes

A black note head with a stem and flag (or beam) attached represents an eighth note. In 4/4, 3/4, or 2/4 time, each eighth note is equivalent to one half of a beat. Therefore, two eighth notes are required to fill the span of one beat. The example below shows eighth notes connected by beams. In this example there are four eighth notes attached to a beam. It is also very common to see eighth notes beamed in pairs, thereby indicating that they are part of the same beat.

Music Notation Symbols — Durations of Rests

Symbols showing the duration of rests are counted in the same manner as notes. The difference is that there is no sound to be sustained over the specified duration.

Whole Rest
Do not play any note for the duration of four beats.

Half Rest
Rest during beats one and two. Play on beats three and four.

45

Quarter Rests

Play on beats one and three. Rest on beats two and four.

count: 1   2   3   4

Eighth Rests

Eighth rests do not have beams. Each eighth note rest stands alone. Single eighth notes have flags instead of beams. Play notes on the beats and stop the string from sounding between the beats by placing a right-hand finger on the string. When the right-hand finger stops the string from sounding it is prepared to play the note on the next beat.

count: 1   &   2   &   3   &   4   &

The Tie and the Dotted Half Note

The tie is a curved line that connects two notes of the same pitch and combines their durations. Only the first note of the tied pair is struck and the note is held through the duration of the second note. In measure one below, the open B is played on beat one and rings through beat three. A quarter note is played on beat four. In the second measure, the dotted half note is equivalent to three beats in 4/4 time. That is the same duration as the first note of measure one. Therefore, the rhythms shown in measures one and two are identical. A tie can also extend the duration of a note over a barline or over several barlines. In measure three, the first note rings through beats one, two, and three and then a quarter note is played that rings over the barline through beat one.

count: 1   (2   3)   4   1   (2   3)   4   1   (2   3)   4   (1)   2   (3   4)

Musical Expression Symbols

Musical expression symbols specify the relative volume of notes, timbre (quality of sound: bright, dark, etc.), articulation, tempo (frequency of the pulse or beat), mood, etc. Here are some basic musical expression symbols:

Volume

ffff — fortissississimo (very, very, very loud)

fff — fortississimo (very, very loud)

ff — fortissimo (very loud)

f — forte (loud)

mf — mezzo forte (medium loud)

mp — mezzo-piano (medium soft)

p — piano (soft)

pp — pianissimo (very soft)

ppp — pianississimo (very, very soft)

pppp — pianissississimo (very, very, very soft)

Tempo

Largo — very slow (40-60 beats per minute)

Larghetto — A little faster than largo (60-66 bpm)

Adagio — slow (66-76 bpm)

Andante — walking pace (76-108 bpm)

Moderato — moderate (108-120 bpm)

Allegro — happy, fast (120-168 bpm)

Presto — very fast (168-200 bpm)

Prestissimo — very, very, fast (200 bpm. or faster)

Ritard (Ritardando) — to gradually slow the tempo or to play slowly.

Accelerando — to gradually speed up the tempo or play faster.

Timbre (Tone Quality)

Dolce — Sweetly (Right hand over the soundhole)

Normal — Normal (Right hand 1-3 cm behind the sound hole)

Ponticello — Near the bridge producing a bright, thin, nasal sound.

Articulation

Staccato — play the note short, or detached from the other notes with silence in between notes. Indicated by a dot similar to a period placed above or below the note head.

Tenuto — to hold the note slightly longer than normal, indicated by a dash similar to a hyphen (–) placed over the note.

Legato — a smooth connection between the notes in a melody.

The Musical Alphabet

The term **pitch** refers to the highness or lowness of a sound. The alphabetical letters A through G may be found in different **registers**. A register is the approximate range of an instrument or vocalist. A bass vocalist sings in a lower register than a soprano. A string bass (double bass) plays in a lower register than a violin. Each of these instruments is capable of playing the alphabetically designated pitches A through G, but they do so in different **octaves**. An octave is the duplication of a pitch eight steps higher. This occurs because there are only seven different alphabetical letters in the musical alphabet. When a G is played (the seventh letter above A) the next higher letter is the A once again: A, B, C, D, E, F, G, A, etc.

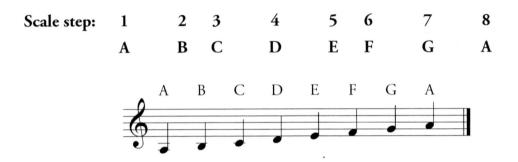

Half Steps and Whole Steps

The adjacent pitches E-F and B-C are only one fret apart on the same string. This interval is called a **natural half step**. All of the other natural adjacent pitches are a **whole step** apart. The interval of a whole step constitutes a distance of two frets apart on the same string. Ex: (A-B) (C-D) (D-E) (F-G) (G-A). **Scale degrees** refer to the position of the note in the scale. If the first note of the scale is "A" the second note of the scale is "B" and so on. In the A pure minor (natural minor) scale, half steps occur between the second and third scale degrees and between the fifth and sixth scale degrees.

The A Pure Minor (Natural Minor) Scale

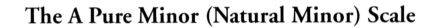

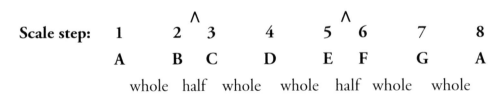

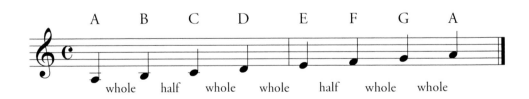

48

The Major Scale

The major scale is composed of the musical pitches named C, D, E, F, G, A, B, C. Because the major scale starts on the pitch "C," the half steps occur between the third and fourth scale degrees and between the seventh and eighth scale degrees.

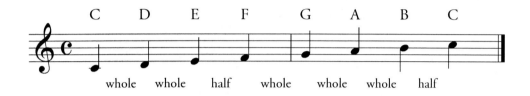

Scale step:	1	2	3	^ 4	5	6	7	^ 8
	C	D	E	F	G	A	B	C

whole   whole half whole whole whole half

C   D   E   F   G   A   B   C

whole   whole half whole whole whole half

THE OPEN TREBLE STRINGS

The notes that represent the open treble strings are shown below:

Open 1st string   Open 2nd string   Open 3rd string

Rhythm Exercises

Prepare the right-hand thumb by placing it on the sixth string. The nail and flesh should make simultaneous contact with the string. The nail and flesh of the index finger of the right hand should also make simultaneous contact with the first string prior to playing the rest stroke.

Play the following exercises with the metronome set to 60 bpm. The quarter note equals one beat, or one click of the metronome. In Example 1, use the right-hand index finger to play the first string open E on beat exactly coinciding with the click of the metronome, allowing the note to ring through beats two, three and four. Then in measure two, play the open E on beat one with the right hand middle finger and allow it to ring through beat two. Play the second half note on beat three and allow it to ring through beat four. Continue to alternate the index and middle fingers in this manner.

It is important to allow all notes to ring for their full duration. This will produce a sound that is smooth and connected, or *legato*. Do not allow them to be cut short by preparing the right-hand fingers too soon. Prepare the right hand a millisecond before it is supposed to play so the notes will not be short and detached, or *staccato*. There are instances when it is musically expressive and appropriate to play staccato but at first, one should learn to play legato.

The Open First String: E

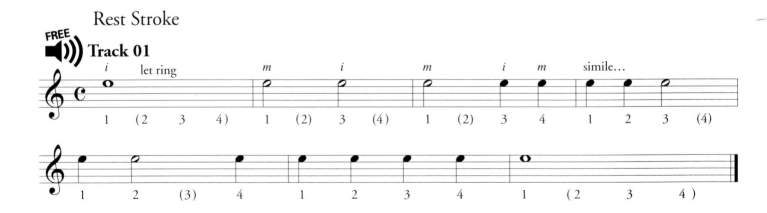

The Open Second String: B

The Open Third String: G

FREE 🔊 Track 06

FREE 🔊 Track 07

The Arpeggio

The term *arpeggio* means "to play in the manner of the harp." The notes of a **chord** (three or more notes sounding together) may be played simultaneously or separately. The purpose of this exercise is to learn to move the fingers of the right hand in the way that is necessary to play chords later in the book.

FREE 🔊 Track 08

FREE 🔊 Track 09

Systematic Arpeggio Exercises

Exercises 10-12 all start with the index finger on the third string. Exercises 14-17 start with the middle finger on the second string. Exercises 18-21 start with the ring finger on the first string. Play and repeat exercises for one minute each. It is possible to prepare each finger very quickly after the previous finger plays without cutting off the duration of the notes. When practicing arpeggio Ex. 10, prepare the index finger on the third string and anchor the thumb on the 6th string in the same manner described earlier. Play a free stroke with the index finger and quickly prepare the middle finger on the 2nd string while the 3rd string is ringing. Then play a free stroke with the *m* finger. Follow this with a quick preparation of the ring finger on the 1st string. Then play a free stroke with the *a* finger on the 1st string. Quickly prepare the *m* finger on the 2nd string these before playing it and then repeat the exercise.

The purpose of these exercises is to create right-hand finger strenth and independence by practicing all of the four-note arpeggio patterns using *i, m, a*. Play each measure for one minute.

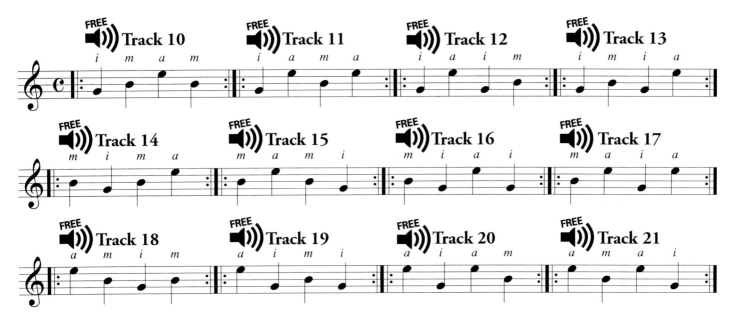

Alternating the Index and Middle Fingers on the Treble Strings

Practice Ex. 22 with right hand finger combinations such as (*i, m*) (*a, m*) (*m, a*) (*i, a*) (*a, i*).

The purpose of this exercise is to improve right-hand finger strength and dexterity in the alternation of two fingers. Using rest stroke, push *i* through the 1st string toward the soundboard; as it makes contact with the 2nd string, *m* plays and *i* simultaneously returns to playing position. As *m* makes contact with the 2nd string *i* plays and *m* simultaneously returns to playing position.

In the following duet, "Sueño," Guitar 1 is played by the student and uses only the open treble strings. Guitar 2 is played by the teacher or an intermediate or advanced guitarist along with the student. The student should listen to the division of the beat being played by Guitar 2 (eighth notes) in order to play the quarter, half, and whole notes precisely on the downbeats. The recording is included in **CD Track 22**.

The purpose of this composition is to learn to play the open treble strings in whole, half, and quarter notes in ensemble with another guitarist. Use rest stroke throughout.

Sueño

THE OPEN BASS STRINGS

Prepare the right hand by placing the index (*i*) finger on the 3rd string, the middle (*m*) finger on the 2nd string, and the ring (*a*) finger on the 1st string. This will stabilize the right hand and prepare the right hand for playing arpeggios with bass notes. The following exercises are played on the open bass strings with the thumb.

55

The Dotted Half Note

The dotted half note receives three beats in 3/4 or 4/4 time. The dot adds one half of the note value of the original note; i.e., one half of a half note is a quarter note. As a half note receives two beats and a quarter note receives one, the duration of the dotted half note is equal to the sum of the two.

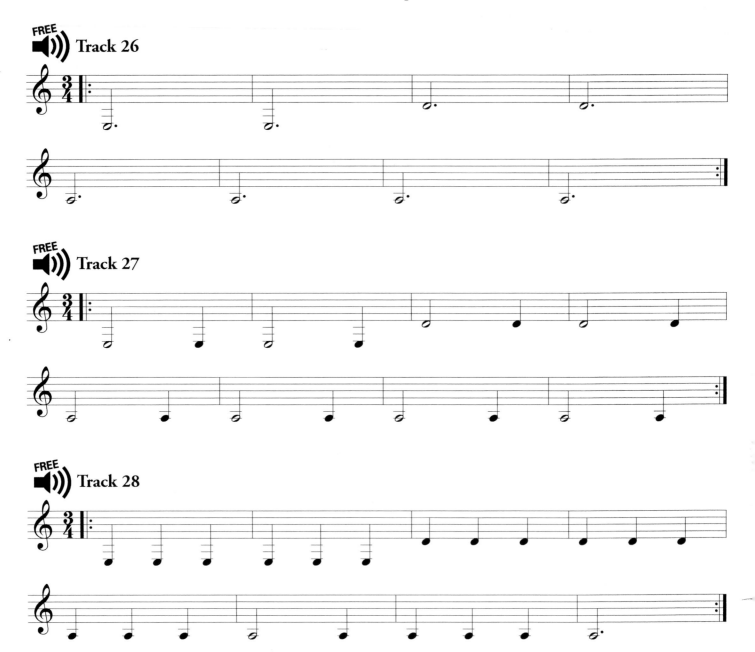

Playing on the Bass and Treble Strings

Exercise 29 is a two-note pattern that requires the thumb and index finger to alternate. Play this exercise with (*p*, *m*) and (*p*, *a*) as well.

The purpose of this exercise is to gain independence in playing with the thumb and fingers in alternation the way they are used in playing melody and bass later in this book. Use free stroke throughout.

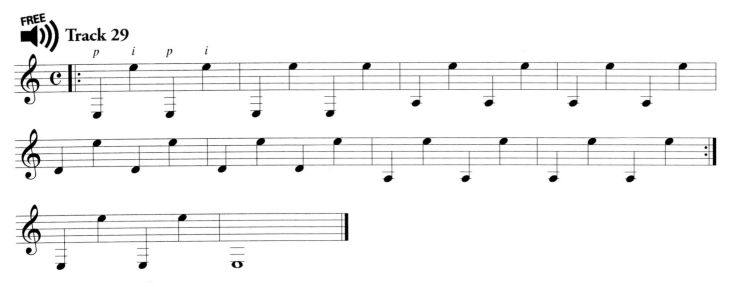

Exercise 30 is a three-note pattern that should be practiced with each of the following finger combinations: (*p, m, i*) (*p, i, m*) (*p, i, a*) (*p, a, i*) (*p, m, a*) and (*p, a, m*).

The purpose of this exercise is to become comfortable playing a three-note pattern consisting of a note on a bass string followed by two melody notes on a treble string. Use free stroke throughout.

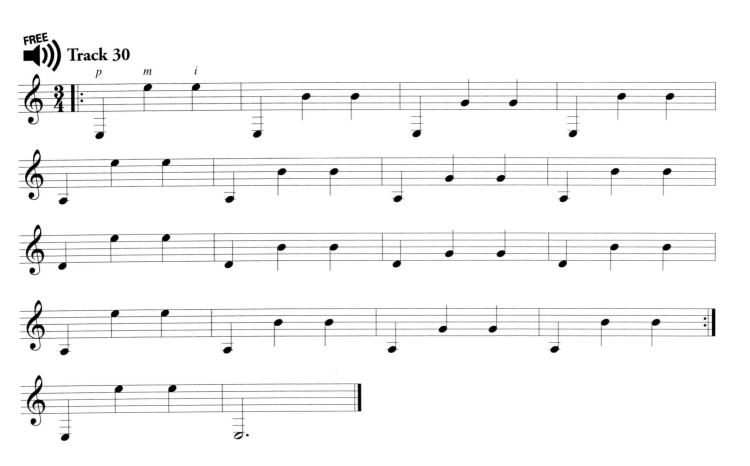

Exercise 31 uses a right-hand pattern that is used in playing bass and melody in alternation. It also serves as a study for arpeggio and **tremolo** technique (a rapid repetition of three or more melodic notes after each bass note). The right-hand pattern for tremolo is (*p, a, m, i*). Also try (*p, i, m, i*) (*p, m, i, m*) (*p, a, m, a*) (*p, m, a, m,*) (*p, i, m, a*) and other combinations.

The purpose of this exercise is to become comfortable playing tremolo while changing between strings.

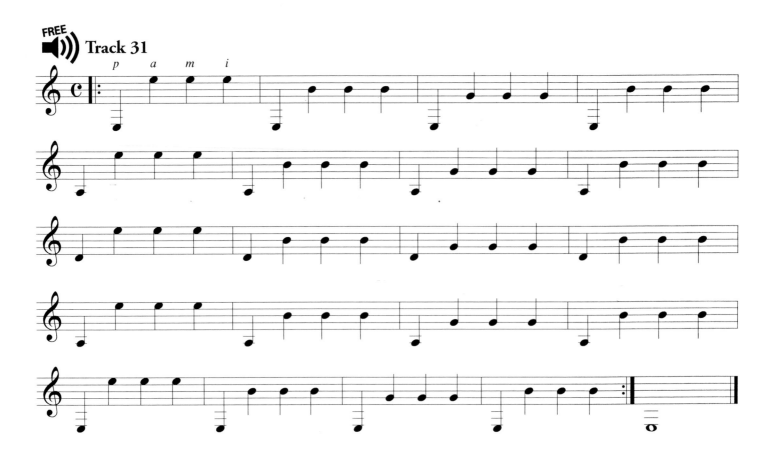

Exercise 32 uses a common right-hand arpeggio pattern. Prepare the thumb on the bass note in each measure and then immediately prepare the other fingers (*a, m, i*) on the treble strings. Play the index without moving the middle finger, then the middle without moving the ring finger before the ring finger finally plays. The thumb then immediately prepares to play the bass note of the next measure to repeat the arpeggio pattern.

Exercises 33–35 use common right-hand patterns for playing arpeggios. In exercise 33, in preparation to play "E," place *p* on the 6th string. Immediately after *p* plays, prepare *a* on the 1st string, etc. This technique is called "consecutive preparation."

In exercise 34, prepare *p* as above and then simultaneously prepare *i, m* and *a* before playing G, B and E. This technique is called "full preparation." After the 1st string E is played, use consecutive preparation before playing *m* and *i*.

FREE 🔊 Track 34

In exercise 35, use consecutive right-hand preparation throughout.

FREE 🔊 Track 35

Exercise 36 helps to develop the right-hand ability to change or cross from one string to another. This is commonly referred to as **string crossing**. This technique is important in playing scales and should be practiced every day as a warm up.

The purpose of this exercise is to improve the right hand's ability to change from one string to another when playing scales later in the book.

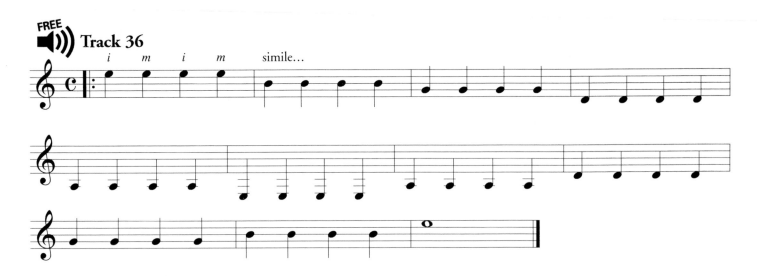

Exercise 37 is a study in playing bass and melody notes in alternation. The melody notes have upward stems and the bass notes have downward stems. Play the melody notes (stems up) with rest stroke and the bass notes (stems down) with free stroke.

The purpose of this exercise is to learn to play rest stroke melody and free stroke bass in alternation and to identify the melody notes by their upward stems.

THE NOTES ON THE FIRST STRING

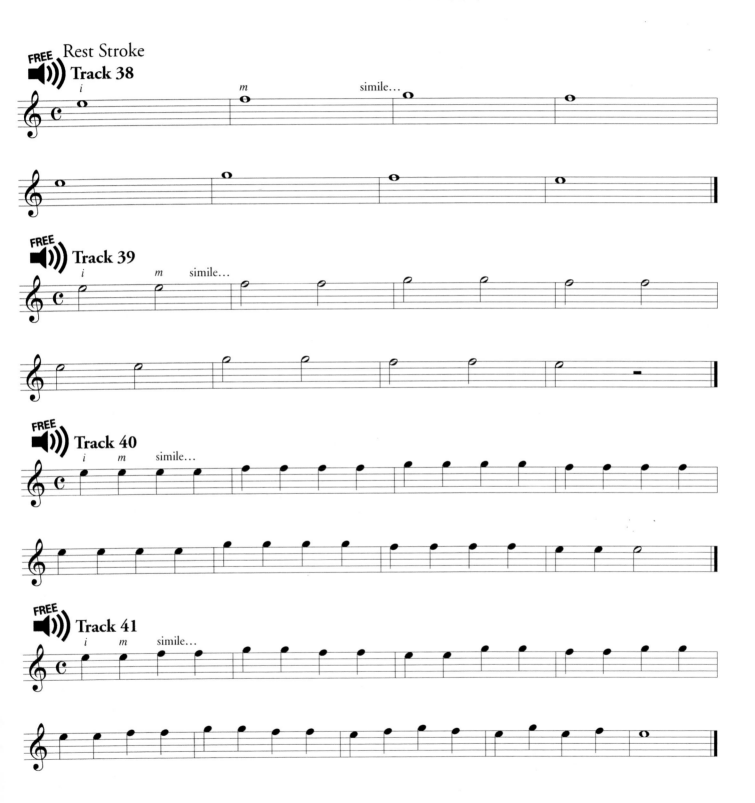

The following duet is for the teacher and student. The student plays Guitar 1 which uses only the notes on the first string, while the teacher plays Guitar 2. Guitar 2 may be played by a student once the chord section of the book has been mastered and the notes in the first position are learned. The purpose of this composition is to learn to play the notes on the first string in the first position using whole, half and quarter notes in ensemble with another guitarist. This duet is also a study in flamenco literature because the Soleares is the mother of all flamenco forms. Learning this form will help the student learn the other flamenco forms more easily. Each phrase is equivalent to 12 beats in common time. The accent pattern is strong on beats 3, 6, 8, 10, and 12. The other beats are relatively weaker. This beat and accent pattern forms the *compás* of the Soleares form (one flamenco compás is equivalent to four classical measures). Each line of music in this composition is four measures long and forms one phrase. The letter "G" inside of the square on beat twelve is the symbol for *golpe*. *Golpe* means to hit or tap the top of the flamenco guitar with the ring finger on the *golpeador* (tap guard). This example is included on **CD Track 41**.

SOLEARES

62

In exercise 42, follow the same directions as for exercise 37. Exercise 42 uses fretted (closed) notes on the first string. The purpose of this exercise is to learn to play melody notes and open bass notes in alternation using quarter notes.

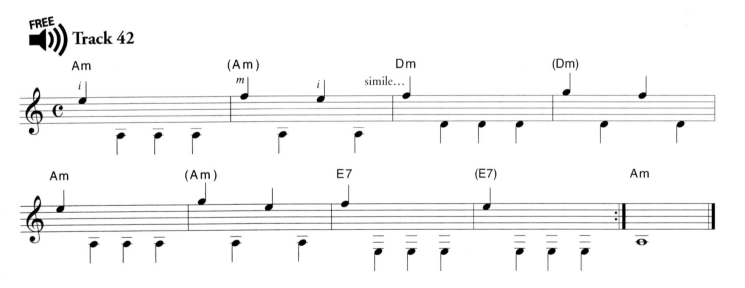

Exercise 43 is similar to exercise 42 but the stems of the melody notes go down. The melody notes are not required to have upward stems. Music in three or more parts may have the melody in a middle or lower voice (part) and the accompaniment may be in a higher register. The purpose of this exercise is to learn to play alternating fretted melody notes and open bass notes in quarter note rhythm.

Track 43

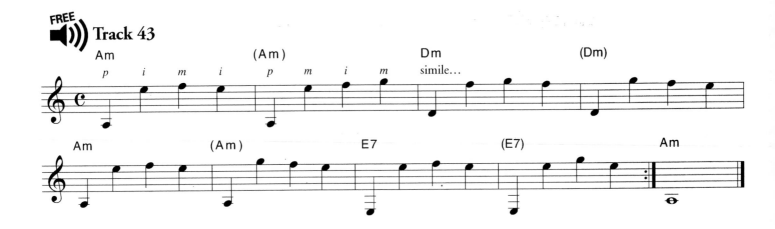

THE NOTES ON THE SECOND STRING

B	C	D
Open	1st fret 1st finger	3rd fret 3rd finger

Rest Stroke

Track 44

Track 45

Track 46

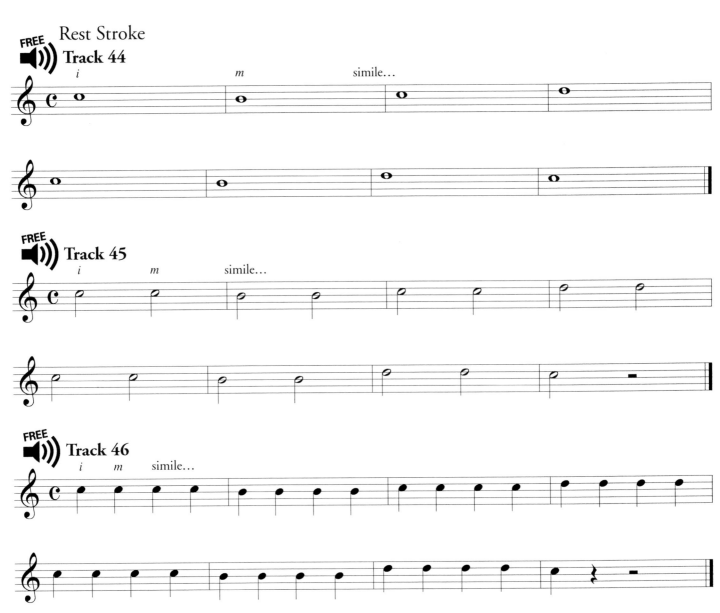

MUSIC IN TWO PARTS
The Individual Parts—Melody and Bass

Melody
The purpose of this exercise is to learn the melody part alone.

Bass
The purpose of this exercise is to learn the bass part alone.

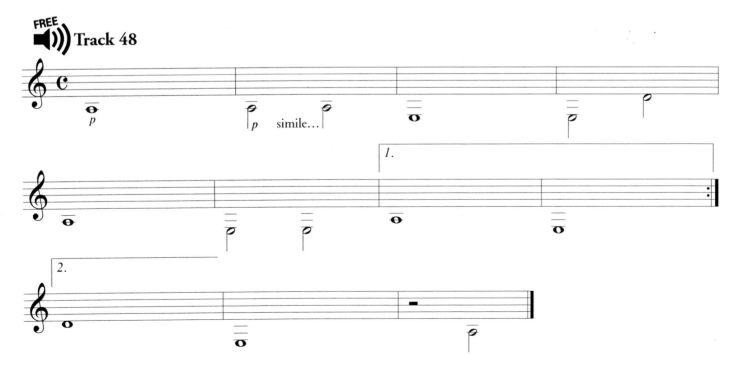

Both Parts Together

The purpose of this exercise is to learn to play the melody and bass parts simultaneously and to learn that separate rests and notes are required for each part.

FREE Track 49

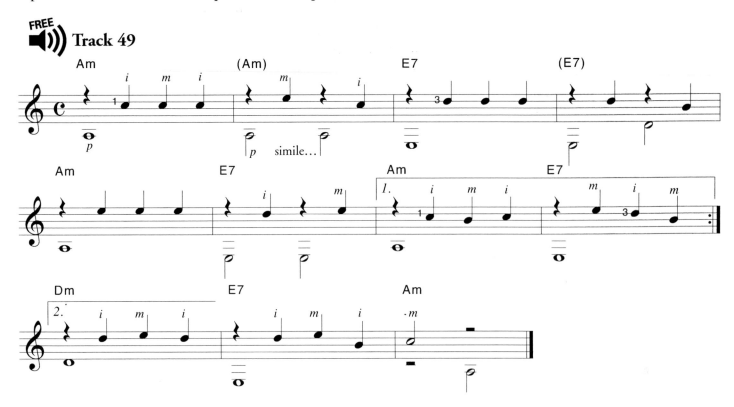

The purpose of this next exercise is to play two parts together. The upper part is an arpeggio used to accompany the lower bass part. The upper notes are not always melodic in nature, sometimes they are simply accompaniment; that is, they form a chord harmony with the bass rather than a melody with the bass. Chords will be explained in detail later.

FREE Track 50

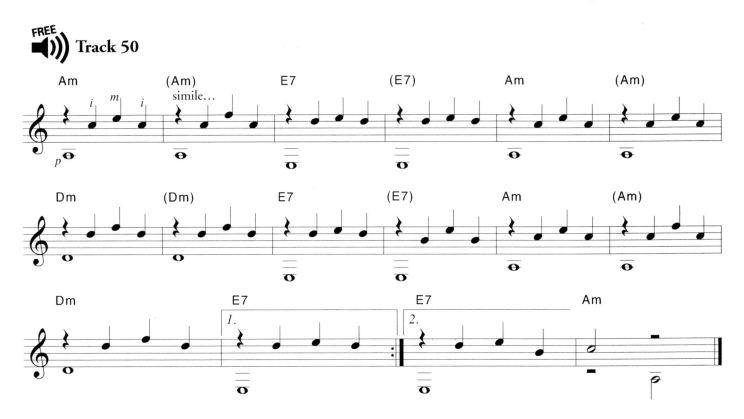

Playing Eighth Notes

Exercise 51 uses the eighth-note division in the fourth measure. The eighth notes either occur with the foot taps (downbeat) or when the foot is at its apex in between taps (upbeat). The division of the beat is shown in measure four using the ampersand (&) for the "and" when you count: 1 and 2 and 3 and 4 and etc. The purpose of this exercise is to learn to play eighth notes in combination with half notes and quarter notes.

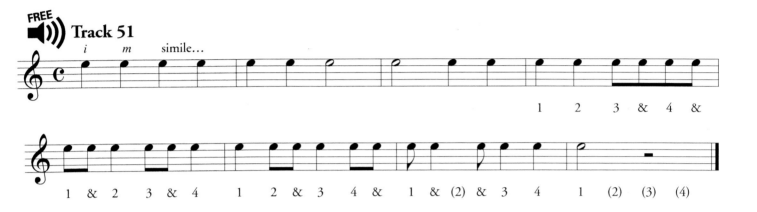

The purpose of exercise 52 is to learn to play eighth notes on both the downbeats and the upbeats. The Arabic numerals in parentheses illustrate where to allow a note to ring or where to stop the note if a rest is present above that number or ampersand symbol, (&). These parentheses should not be confused with the circled string designation numbers that specify the string on which a note should be played, e.g. ⑤–fifth string.

Examples 53-64 show all of the systematic right-hand arpeggio patterns in eighth note rhythm. This exercise helps to improve independence between the fingers of the right hand. Move the fingers only and keep the right hand still as each arpeggio is played. Additionally, the thumb may play a bass string such as the low E string on beat one or on any other beat of the measure to improve independence between the thumb and the other fingers.

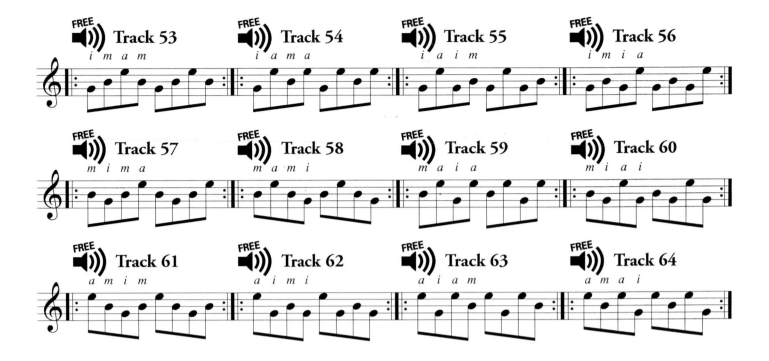

Exercise 65 features the alternation of quarter notes and eighth notes as the right hand changes from one string to another. The purpose of this exercise is to improve right-hand facility in preparation for playing scales. After *i* plays, it exchanges position with *m*, moving into playing position as *m* plays. Similarly an exchange occurs after *m* plays, it returns to playing position as *i* plays.

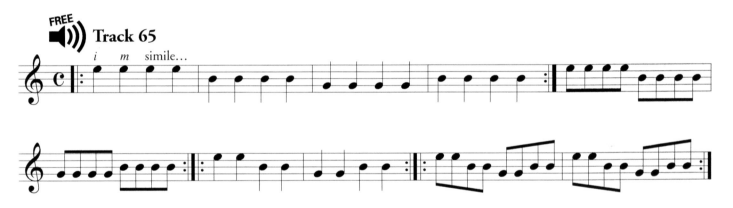

Exercise 66 should be played entirely with the thumb, (*p*). The purpose of this exercise is to practice repeating the thumb on the bass strings and to cross or change strings with the thumb.

The dotted quarter note is equivalent to one pulse or foot tap in $^6_8$ time. The $^6_8$ time signature is classified as compound duple meter (as the six beats are divisible in two groups of three). The difference between $^6_8$ and $^2_4$ time is that $^2_4$ time is regarded as simple meter as each beat is divided into two equal parts. Exercise 67 shows some of the various divisions of the measure and different divisions of the beat in $^6_8$ time. The purpose of this exercise is to learn to play the dotted quarter note rhythm in $^6_8$ time.

6 **beats** to a measure, counted in 2 groups of 3 with accents on 1 and 4.
8 an 8th note gets one beat.

In $^6_8$ the dotted quarter receives 3 beats or one foot tap.

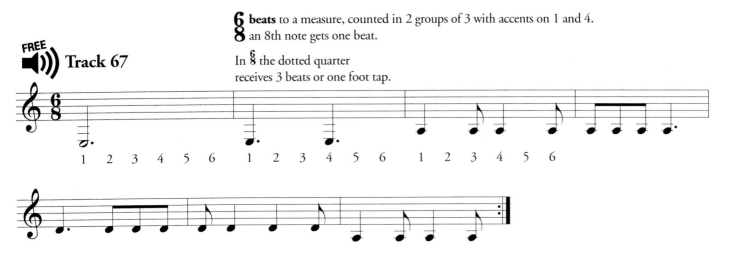

Exercise 68 uses a rhythm called **swing** that is commonly used in American blues and jazz. The purpose of this exercise is to learn to break the dotted quarter note into two (unequal) parts. The first part is a quarter note that fills two thirds of a beat, the second part is an eighth note that fills one third of a beat. While written here in $^6_8$ time, swing music is often written in "straight 8ths" in $^2_4$ or $^4_4$ time with the understanding that they would be played as triplet or "swing 8ths."

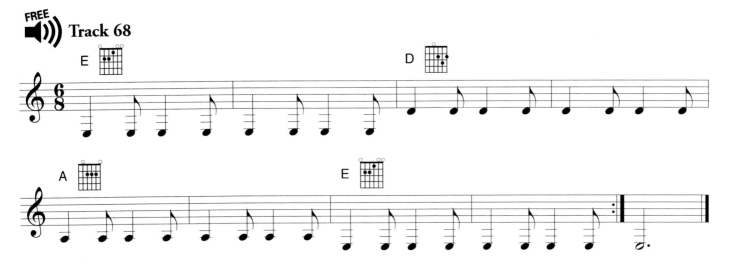

Exercise 69 is a bass line for a 12-bar (12-measure) blues form. The purpose of this exercise is to learn to play the rhythm from Ex. 52 in a complete musical form. The annotations above the staves are chord symbols for the teacher. The chords may be played by the teacher as the student plays the bass part. After the student learns the chords shown later in the book, the chords may be played by a student.

The purpose of Ex. 70 is to use the right-hand scale motion, crossing strings, in eighth-note rhythm. This helps to develop comfort and accuracy in changing strings during scale passages. Practice this exercise with all right-hand finger combinations, [(*i, m*) (*m, i*) (*i, a*) (*a, i*) (*m, a*) (*a, m*)]. This approach develops nearly equal strength and facility in all of the finger combinations that might be used to play scale or melody passages. Play with as much force as possible without creating any tension in the arm, shoulder, back, neck or face. Playing loudly when practicing scales makes them easier to play at any volume in a musical composition.

FREE
Track 70

THE NOTES ON THE THIRD STRING

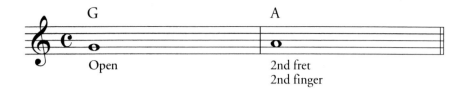

The purpose of learning the following *Sevillanas* melody is to develop the ability to read and play notes on the 1st, 2nd and 3rd strings. The Sevillanas, is a folkloric Spanish dance adopted by flamenco singers, dancers and guitarists. It is traditionally performed as one of a set of four Sevillanas in different **keys**. (Scales, chords, and keys will be explained later in detail.) This Sevillanas uses the notes A, B, C, D, E, F, and G on the first three strings. Use rest stroke to play the notes with the right hand and rest the thumb of the right hand on the 6th string for security and stability.

SEVILLANAS

Track 71

Guitar Part 1 of the "Sevillanas Trio" is the same as the previous exercise. Guitar 2 is a harmonization of that melody and Guitar 3 is a harmonization on open bass strings. The *salida* is the melodic part that signals the dancers to depart from the introduction and begin the *copla*. The copla is the melody that must be repeated three times in order to complete the Sevillanas I.

Examples of other Sevillanas can be found in *Flamenco Guitar: Basic Techniques, Sabor Flamenco and Systematic Studies for Flamenco Guitar* by Juan Serrano. The Sevillanas was also adopted by Spanish Nationalist composers such as Isaac Albéniz in Sevilla (Sevillanas) from *Suite Española Op. 47*. Although the Sevillanas of Albéniz is much different than the flamenco Sevillanas, it has the same time signature, similar tempo, and uses key changes within a single composition. The Sevilla (Sevillanas) of Albéniz is often choreographed by flamenco and classical dancers.

SEVILLANAS I

Juan Serrano

Sharps and Flats on the 1st, 2nd and 3rd strings

The sharp symbol (♯) placed before a note on the staff raises the pitch of that note by one half step; placing the flat symbol (♭) before a note on the staff lowers that note by one half step. The pitches on the guitar fretboard get higher in pitch as they approach the body of the instrument. In order to play one half step higher, move one fret further toward the body on the same string.

Two notes that are spelled differently but sound the same pitch are said to be *enharmonic*. These notes are played on the same string and fret. The sharp and flat notes on the 1st, 2nd and 3rd strings are shown below. Notes that appear in the same measure below are enharmonic pairs and are played at the same string and fret location.

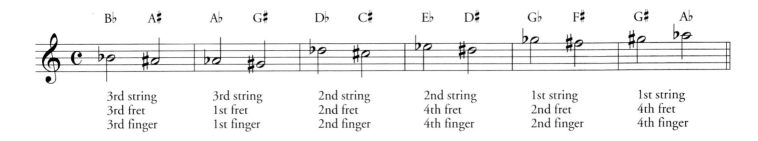

3rd string		3rd string		2nd string		2nd string		1st string		1st string
3rd fret		1st fret		2nd fret		4th fret		2nd fret		4th fret
3rd finger		1st finger		2nd finger		4th finger		2nd finger		4th finger

The Fifth Position on the First String

The fifth position on the first string on the guitar fretboard includes frets 5, 6, 7, and 8. Referring to the fretboard chart, find the pitches A, B♭ (A♯), B, and C. These notes are played with the 1st finger at the 5th fret, 2nd finger at the 6th fret, 3rd finger at the 7th fret and the 4th finger at the 8th fret.

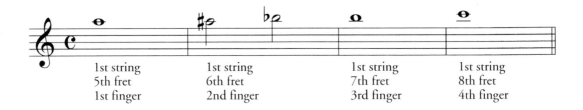

1st string	1st string	1st string	1st string
5th fret	6th fret	7th fret	8th fret
1st finger	2nd finger	3rd finger	4th finger

The Natural Sign

Sharps and flats remain in effect throughout a measure without being rewritten if the same note appears more than once in that measure. The effect of a sharp symbol or flat symbol is canceled by the use of a natural sign or the occurance of a bar line.

The Natural cancels the sharp; the Bar Line also cancels the sharp

C-sharp	C-natural	C-sharp	C-natural

ROMANZA IN A MINOR

Track 73

ROMANZA

The melody has been harmonized with open-string bass notes. Play rest strokes on all notes with upward stems and free strokes on all bass notes (downward stems).

FARRUCAS

This "Farrucas" by Juan Serrano will help you learn to play the C♯ on the 2nd string and the G♯ on the 3rd string in a musical form that is very common in flamenco. The Farrucas is in common time and contains phrases that are equivalent to 8 beats or two measures. This melody might accompany a flamenco dancer and could be harmonized with other notes or chords played by other guitarists.

Track 75

Sixteenth Notes

Sixteenth notes divide a single beat into four equal parts. The first sixteenth note falls on the downbeat (1). The second sixteenth note falls on the syllable "ee" (e), the third falls on "and" (&), and the last falls on the syllable "uh" (a). The second beat starts by counting the number "2" followed by the same syllables counted in beat one.

1 e & a 2 e & a 3 e & a 4 e & a

Slurs

The slur is an articulation technique used to place an emphasis on one note and less emphasis on another. It is notated in music by a curved line connecting two notes of a different pitch. The slur is executed by picking a note with the right hand as usual and then playing a subsequent note that is either higher or lower in pitch by using the left hand instead of the right. When a lower note follows the picked note, a left-hand finger must **pull-off** to play the lower note. This is called a **descending slur** or **legato**. When a note of higher pitch follows the picked note, the left hand must **hammer-on** the string to play the higher note. This is called an **ascending slur** or **legato**.

In the example below, the first ascending slur occurs from the note "G" to the note "A." The "G" is played on the open third string by the right hand picking the note, and the "A" is played by hammering on the second fret of the same string with the second finger of the left hand. The second ascending slur occurs from the note "C" to the note "C♯" on the second beat. The "C" is played on the first fret of the second string, plucked by the first finger of the right hand. The "C♯" is played by hammering on the second fret of the same string with the second finger.

1 e & a 2 e & a

Playing the melody of "Estudio No. 2" will help you become familiar with playing D♯ on the second string, the use the ascending slur, reading sixteenth notes, and producing a quality sound with the rest stroke. In addition, the student can further develop the ability to alternate the index and middle fingers of the right hand. Focus on the quality of the sound the right hand is producing; eliminate any clicking sound made by the right-hand fingernails by being sure that the nail and the fleshy part of the fingertip make simultaneous contact with the string. Push slightly inward toward the soundboard of the guitar as each finger performs the rest stroke.

ESTUDIO NO.2

Fernando Sor

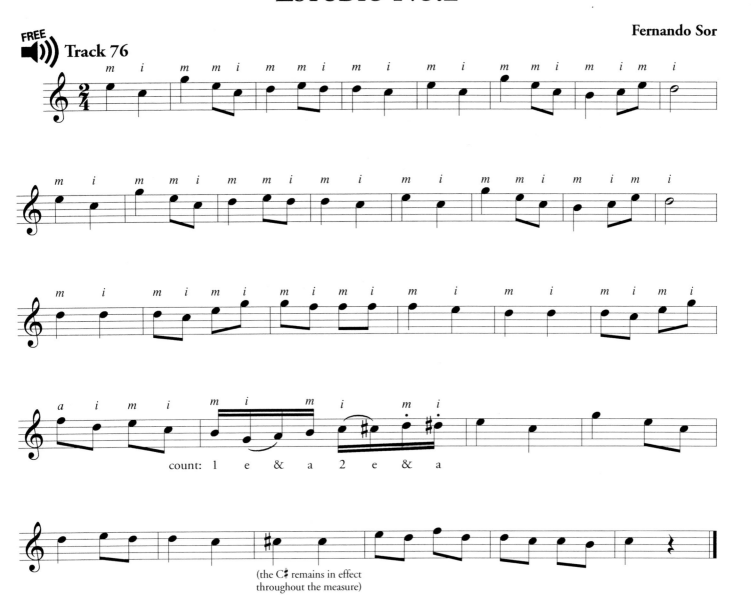

(the C♯ remains in effect
throughout the measure)

"Estudio No. 2" is the second of twenty studies for the guitar selected for an edition by Andrés Segovia. This study comes from a larger group of studies by Fernando Sor, but is called "Estudio No. 2" in the Segovia edition. In the following arrangement, the second part is for the teacher to play along with the student. The purpose of this duet is to learn to play the melody of an important study in the classical guitar repertoire, and to prepare the student for further study of the composition arranged for solo guitar. Listen to the bass notes of the lower part to maintain synchronicity between the parts and limit any confusion that might be caused by the sixteenth notes played in the lower part.

ESTUDIO No.2
Duet

Fernando Sor

THE MAJOR SCALE

The model scale for major scales is composed of the musical pitches C, D, E, F, G, A. B, C. Because the major scale starts on the pitch "C," the natural half steps occur between the third and fourth scale degrees and between the seventh and eighth scale degrees.

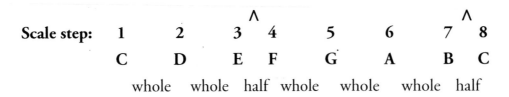

Scale step:	1	2	3	4	5	6	7	8
	C	D	E	F	G	A	B	C
		whole	whole	half	whole	whole	whole	half

Playing the Major Scale

The **C major scale** starts on the note "C" and ascends though the musical alphabet past "G," then continues ascending through "A" and "B," finally arriving on "C"- eight letters above the original note. This is a one-octave scale because it ascends through the alphabet arriving on the same letter (note) one octave higher. The locations of all of the pitches in the C major scale are shown in the first position. The C Major Scale is shown here in one octave on the 1st and 2nd strings in whole notes, half notes, quarter notes, eighth notes, and sixteenth notes. The notes A, B, and C are played in the 5th position. The note names are shown below. Notice that the half steps occur between scale degrees three and four and also between scale degrees seven and eight. "Estudio No. 2" by Fernando Sor uses the C Major Scale. This scale is commoly used in music written for the guitar and should be memorized so that the scale can be played without looking at the fretboard.

Important tip: Place your music on the music stand to the left of your chair so that the music is in the same line of sight as your left hand. That way, while keeping your eyes on the music, the left hand is visible in your peripheral vision.

The music should only be used until the scale is memorized. Make sure to alternate two fingers of the right hand when playing the scale. Play the scale with all possible combinations of the right-hand fingers: (*i*, *m*) (*m*, *i*) (*i*, *a*) (*a*, *i*) (*a*, *m*) (*m*, *a*). Repeat each example as many times as necessary and always end on the note "C."

FREE Track 77

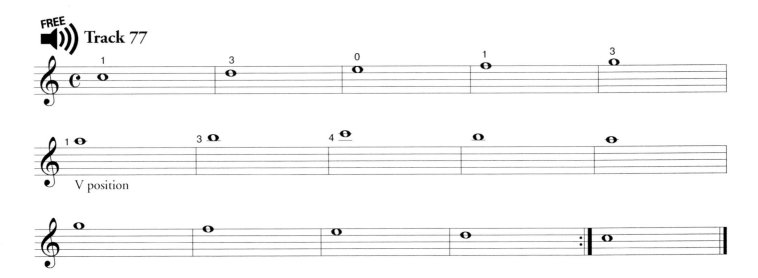

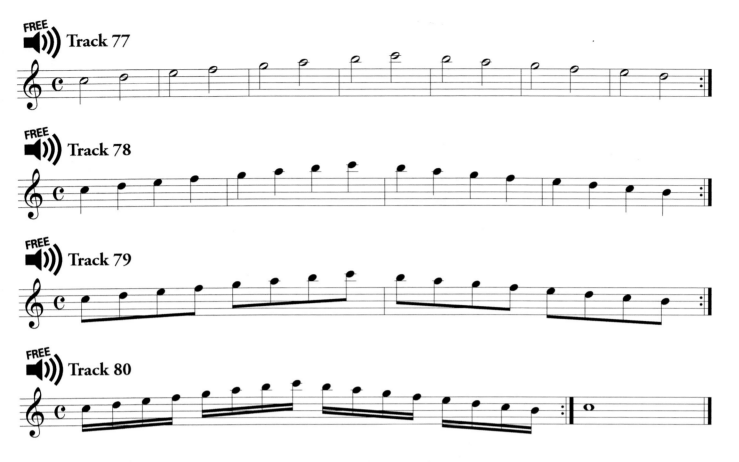

Track 77

Track 78

Track 79

Track 80

THE NATURAL (RELATIVE) MINOR SCALE

As the C major scale and the A natural minor scale share the same pitches, the A natural minor scale is said to be the **relative minor** of the C major scale. Conversely, the C major scale is the **relative major** of the A natural minor scale. The model scale for the natural (pure) minor scale is composed of the musical pitches: A, B, C, D, E, F, G, A.

The A Pure Minor Natural Minor Scale

Scale step:	1	2	3	4	5	6	7	8
	A	B	C	D	E	F	G	A

whole half whole whole half whole whole

Playing the Natural (Relative) Minor Scale

Learn the location of the pitches of the natural minor scale on the open strings and the first three frets (also see fretboard diagram). The **A natural minor scale** has no sharps (♯) or flats (♭). Left-hand fingers are numbered as follows: 1=index, 2=middle, 3=ring, 4=pinky (little). Play each scale with all right-hand finger combinations. The half steps occur between scale degrees (2-3) and (5-6). The A minor scale is used in the Sevillanas, Fandango, and Greensleeves. Practice all possible fingerings for the right hand repeat each example as many times as necessary and always end on the note "A."

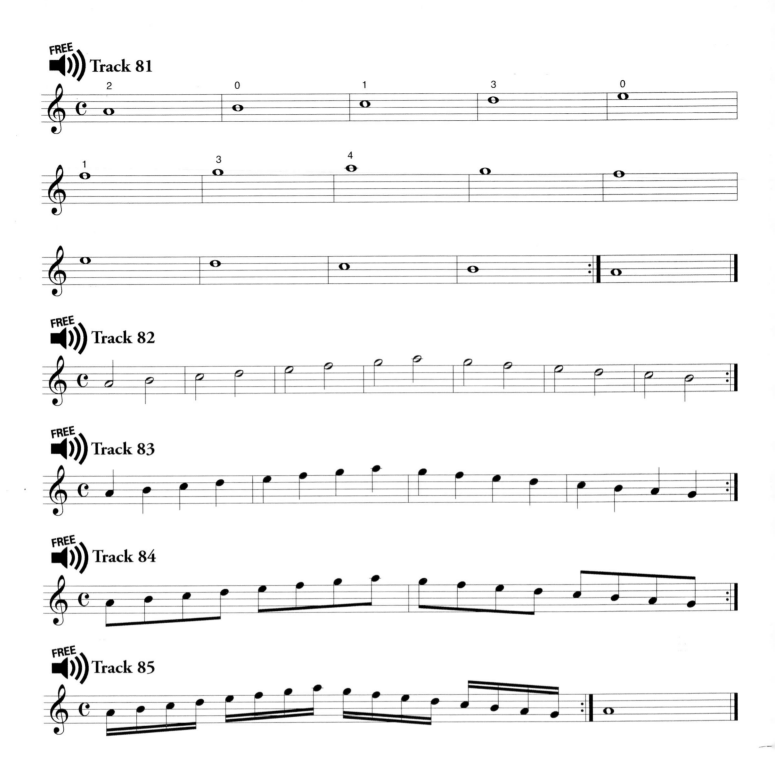

THE A HARMONIC MINOR SCALE

The **A harmonic minor scale** has a raised 7th scale degree; notice that the G is raised a half step to G♯. The G♯ on the 1st string is at the fourth fret and played with the fourth finger. The G♯ on the third string is at the first fret and is played with the first finger. The half steps occur between scale degrees (2-3), (5-6), and (7-8). The interval of one-and-a-half steps that occurs between the sixth and seventh scale degrees gives this scale a Middle-Eastern sound quality. This scale is used in the Farrucas.

Scale step:	1	2	3	4	5	6	7	8
	A	B	C	D	E	F	G♯	A
	whole	half	whole	whole	half	(1+½)	half	

85

THE A MELODIC MINOR SCALE

The **A Melodic Minor Scale** has raised 6th and 7th scale degrees on the ascent, reverting to the pure minor form on the descent with the 6th and 7th lowered to their original places. The ascending portion of the melodic minor scale is the only difference between this scale and the natural (pure) minor scale. The half steps occur between scale steps (2-3) and (7-8) on the ascent, and revert to (2-3) and (5-6) on the descent.

Melodic Minor (Ascending)

Scale step:	1	2	3	4	5	6	7	8
	A	B	C	D	E	F♯	G♯	A
	whole	half	whole	whole	whole	whole	half	

Important note: Accidentals (sharps, ♯, or flats, ♭, not included in the key signature), affect a note through a complete measure. A barline effectively cancels the effect of an accidental. For example, the sharps in measures 6-7 of the following exercise are cancelled in measures 9-10 by barlines. Also, in Ex. 91-93 the last note is made sharp because the next note is "A." This is common practice, in a minor key, when the scale descends past the 1st note of the scale to the 7th degree.

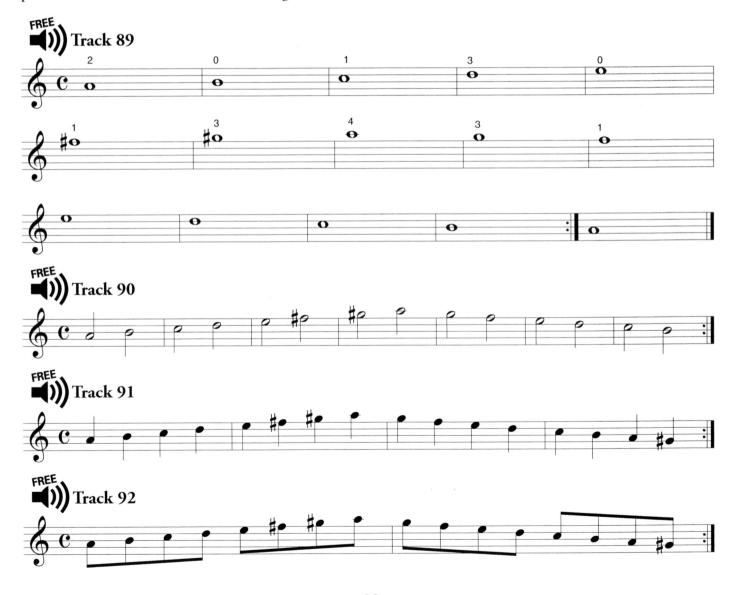

THE CHROMATIC SCALE

Now let's learn the **chromatic scale** on each individual string from the open string to the 12th fret and back to the open string. The chromatic scale is constructed entirely in half steps. It is spelled using sharps (♯) on the ascent and using flats (♭) on the descent. The notes F-sharp (F♯) and G-flat (G♭) are played on the same fret and have the same **pitch** but are spelled differently. Again, when two different note names identify the same pitch, they are said to be enharmonic.

Play each note four times. There are twelve half-steps in the chromatic scale. Each scale degree is numbered below the note names. The distance between all adjacent pitches is one half-step. There are twelve half-steps in the chromatic scale. In the example below, the chromatic scale is shown in both sharp spellings and flat spellings, depending on whether ascending or descending (See example 2).

	^	^	^	^	^	^	^	^	^	^	^	^	
	E	F	F♯	G	G♯	A	A♯	B	C	C♯	D	D♯	E
	E	F	G♭	G	A♭	A	B♭	B	C	D♭	D	E♭	E
Scale step:	1	2	3	4	5	6	7	8	9	10	11	12	(1)
	half	half	half	half	half	half	half	half	half	half	half	half	

Example 1
Playing the Chromatic Scale (Ascending)

String:	⑥												
Fret:	0	1	2	3	4	5	6	7	8	9	10	11	12
Pitch Name (Ascending):	E	F	F♯	G	G♯	A	A♯	B	C	C♯	D	D♯	E
L.H. Finger:	0	1	2	3	4	1	2	3	4	1	2	3	4

Example 2
Playing the Chromatic Scale (Descending)

String:	⑥												
Fret:	12	11	10	9	8	7	6	5	4	3	2	1	0
Pitch Name (Ascending):	E	E♭	D	D♭	C	B	B♭	A	A♭	G	G♭	F	E
L.H. Finger:	4	3	2	1	4	3	2	1	4	3	2	1	0

Learn to play the chromatic scale on each string and become familiar with the note names on each fret of each string both in flat spellings and sharp spellings. Refer to the fretboard diagram.

Notes on the Fourth String

D	E	F
	2nd fret	3rd fret
Open	2nd finger	3rd finger

Fourth String Exercises

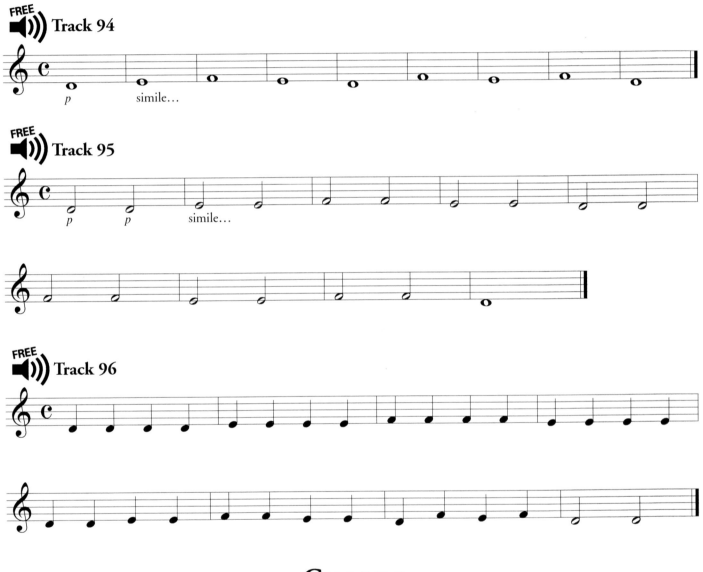

Track 94

p   simile…

Track 95

p   *p*   simile…

Track 96

Chords

A **chord** is defined as three or more different notes sounding together. The last four beats of the Fandango require the performer to play four notes together simultaneously. This harmony or chord is called "E Major." Two notes are fingered (E, G♯) and two are open (B, E). The "E" is pressed with the 2nd finger and the "G♯" is pressed by the 1st finger. Press directly on the fingertips so that the fingers of the left hand do not make contact with adjacent strings, thereby stopping their sound from ringing for the full duration of the notes.

Play all four notes with a rapid downstroke of the thumb. From now on, this technique will be marked in the score with the marking "rasg." for *rasgueado* or "strum."

FANDANGO

The fandango is an important musical form in classical and flamenco styles. This is a flamenco form of the Fandango de Huelva. This form exhibits the Andalucian cadence Am-G-F-E.

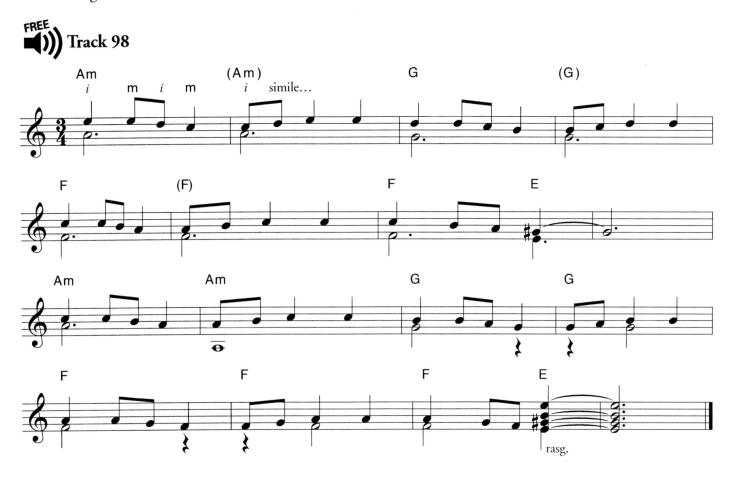

Track 98

This following duet arrangement has a **harmonization** of the melody in the 2nd guitar part. The harmonized part uses the same scale, but does not play the same pitches as the 1st guitar. The notes **harmonize** with one another by making a **consonant**, pleasing sound rather than a **dissonant**, harsh sound. **Consonance** and **dissonance** are equally important in music but in most music, dissonance is used carefully and with observation of certain rules of music composition and theory. The harmonization in "Fandango Duo" is strictly consonant. Try to play precisely together with the 2nd guitar and keep a steady pulse internally by counting three (3/4 time) beats aloud before starting to play together.

FANDANGO DUO

Track 98

Juan Serrano

Notes on the Fifth String

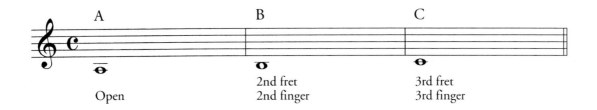

Fifth String Exercises

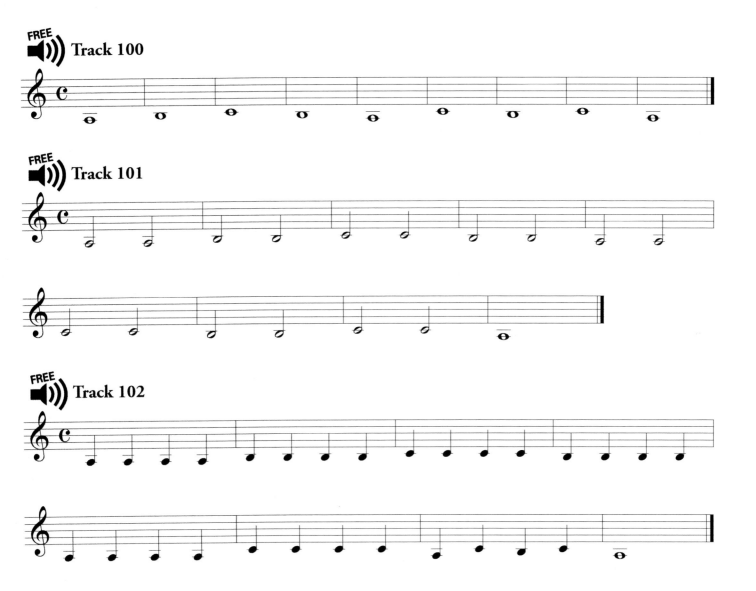

91

HISTORIA DE UN AMOR

This piece uses the A harmonic minor scale. New notes are the "E" on the 4th string as well as the "B" on the 5th string. It is important to focus on the smooth transition from playing with the thumb of the right hand to playing with the fingers. Use rest strokes with the thumb and fingers and focus on producing a beautiful sound. Make sure the fingernails are filed and sanded smooth and push inward toward the top of the guitar as the rest stroke is played.

Track 103

The Dotted Quarter Note

The dotted quarter note receives one and a half beats in common time. The dot adds one half of the original note value.

1 (2) & 3 (4) &   1 & (2) 3 & (4)   1 2 3 (4) &   1 (2) & 3 4   1 2 (3) & 4

Playing the C Major Chord

Measure ten of this piece contains the same chord as at the end of the Fandango, E Major. There is a new chord in the last measure called "C Major." The "C" on the fifth string is played with the third finger. The "E" on the fourth string is played with the second finger, and the "C" on the second string is played with the first finger. The "G" is played on the open string.

PERFIDIA

Alberto Domínguez

Notes on the Sixth String

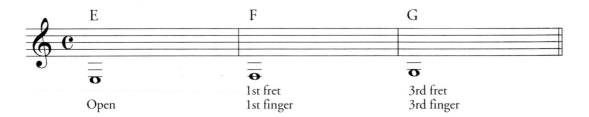

Sixth String Exercises

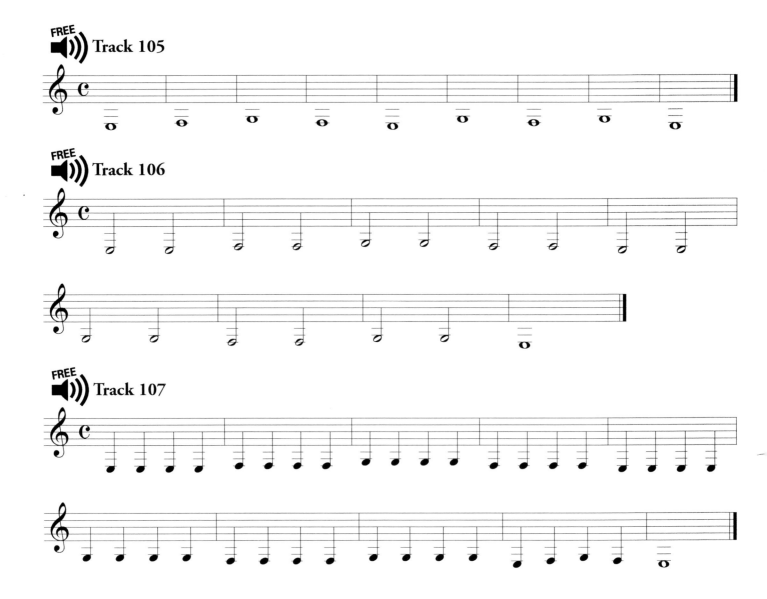

94

Farrucas (Bass Line)

The Farrucas bass line should be played entirely with rest strokes of the right-hand thumb. Always use the 1st finger of the left hand for a note at the first fret, the 2nd finger for a note at the 2nd fret, and the 3rd finger for a note at the 3rd fret.

The following trio can be played by three students and is effective as a good study in ensemble performance. All three guitarists must play precisely together on the beats, and play in tune with a quality sound coming from their instruments. Be careful not to press too hard with the left hand and cause the notes to be out of tune. Also, press the strings down vertically toward the fretboard with the left hand, without pulling them downward toward the floor. Count out four beats before starting to play.

FARRUCAS

Juan Serrano

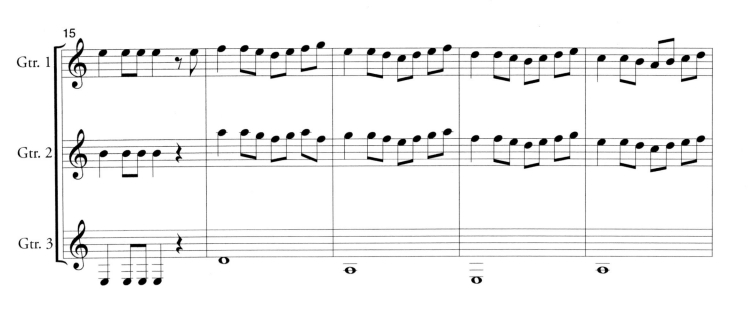

EL ZORONGO
(Bass Line)

The E Major chord at the end of "El Zorongo" is the same as at the end of the Fandango, except that the E Major chord found here uses all six strings. The additional notes are the open "E" and the "B" at the 2nd fret of the fifth string played with the 2nd finger.

The bass line for "El Zorongo" (a popular Spanish song) uses the note "F" on the 6th string in addition to bass notes E, G, A and B. Play all of the notes with a rest stroke of the thumb (*p*). The final E Major chord should be played with a quick downstroke of the thumb so that the notes sound simultaneously. Both this bass line and the following melody offer studies in the use of the tie.

Track 110

EL ZORONGO
(Melody)

The melody for "El Zorongo" includes the bass part at the end of the higher melodic part at the beginning. There is a four-string version of the E major chord in the first section and the full E major chord at the end. This piece presents a study in playing notes in the first position on all six strings. While this piece uses the A harmonic minor scale, it starts and ends on the E major chord. When a piece of music does not start and end on the first note or tonic of a particular scale, it does not use a major or minor scale in the usual way and is not considered to be in a particular key. Rather, it is in a **mode** of the scale or key. The mode used here is common in flamenco and the Spanish nationalist style of classical music. It is one of the three forms of the

Phrygian Dominant Mode:

        Ex. 1 (E F G A B C D E) phrygian mode.
        Ex. 2 (E F G♯ A B C D E) phrygian dominant mode.
        Ex. 3 (E F G G♯ A B C D E) eight-tone Spanish phrygian scale.

However, in the "deep song" or cante hondo of flamenco music, the scale always descends from highest to lowest as in Greek music. The Greek Doric scale descended from A-G-F-E-D-C-B-A-G-F-E-D-C-B-A. The outermost strings of the lyre were tuned to high "e" and low "E." Therefore the characteristic octave of the instrument was a from the high "e" to the low "E." Therefore the descending scale in the characteristic octave was E-D-C-B-A-G-F-E . The last four notes in descending order are what is called "the Andalucian cadence" by Manolo Sanlúcar, (A-G-F-E).

El Zorongo (Melody)

Track 111

EL VITO

Playing the F Major Chord

The F Major chord appears in the fourth measure of the fifth line of "El Vito." The "F" is played with the 3rd finger at the 3rd fret of the 4th string. The "A" is played with the 2nd finger at the 2nd fret of the 3rd string. The "C" is played with the 1st finger at the 1st fret of the 2nd string. Be careful to press straight down on the fingertips so the adjacent strings are not muted.

Playing Two Notes Together (Double Stops)

Prior to the chords in "El Vito," you'll find pairs of notes played simultaneously on adjacent strings. These are called **double stops**. There are pairs of notes played together on non-adjacent strings in measures 34-37. In the measure 34 the "A" bass note is played on beat one with the "B" on the 2nd string. The bass note is held through the second beat as the melody note changes to "C" on beat two. On beat three, "E" and "G" are played together. The bass note "G" is held over the bar line through the second beat of measure 35. The melody note changes to "B" on the first beat of the second measure. Similar motion occurs across the next bar line as the "F" bass note is held in a similar way as the melody note changes from "C" to "A." The passage or phrase ends as the melody moves to "G♯" and the bass moves to "E" on the third beat of measure 36. These notes are held over the bar line through beat one and then they are replaced by the 4th string "E" bass note on beat two of measure 37. "El Vito" is a popular Spanish song that is used in a famous Spanish opera by Geronimo Jimenez.

EL VITO

101

Rasgueado

Rest the thumb on the 4th string and strike the treble strings quickly with the back of the fingernails in the way described at the beginning of the book in the section on rasgueado (see p.36). Repeat each example for 30 seconds and then end on the C major chord. Increase the duration of this exercise by 10 seconds each week until each example is repeated for 3 minutes.

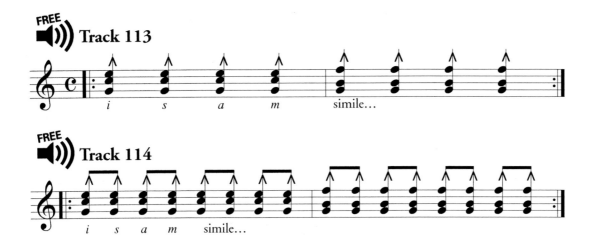

Sevillanas Intro

The Sevillanas intro helps to prepare the student to play the solo version of Sevillanas.

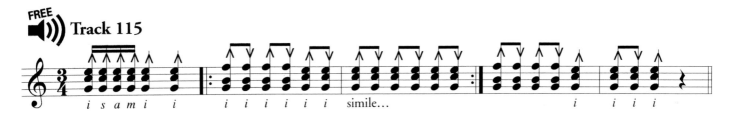

The Natural Notes

The next exercise uses all of the natural notes learned so far, in the first position on strings ① – ⑥ and also the fifth position on the first string.

Sharps and Flats on the Bass Strings

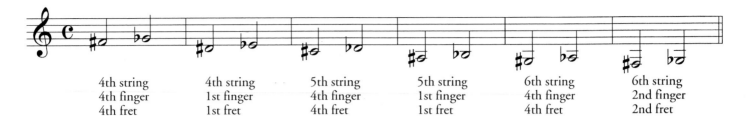

4th string	4th string	5th string	5th string	6th string	6th string
4th finger	1st finger	4th finger	1st finger	4th finger	2nd finger
4th fret	1st fret	4th fret	1st fret	4th fret	2nd fret

The Chromatic Scale

FREE Track 117

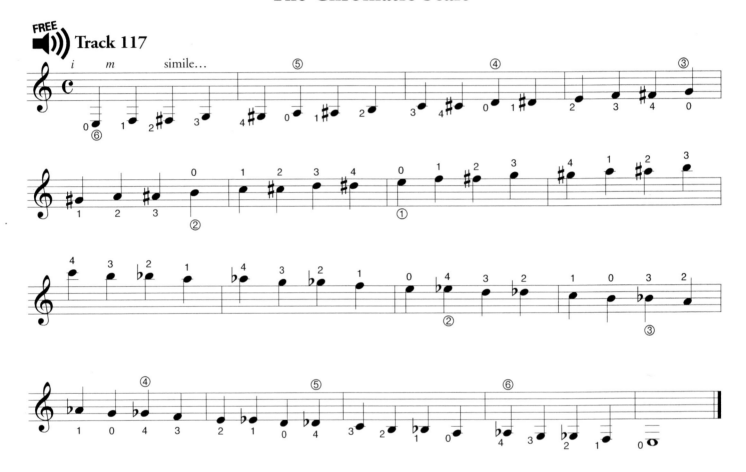

Exercise — Writing the Finger Numbers and String Numbers in the Music

Write the finger number (1, 2, 3, 4) and the string number (①, ②, ③, ④, ⑤, ⑥) next to each note in the music. "El Rancho Grande" is a popular Mexican folksong that uses "F♯" on the 6th and 4th strings.

EL RANCHO GRANDE

Alternating Bass and Chord Progression

Two students can play this duo once they have studied the following section on chords. For now, it should be played by the teacher and student. The bass notes of each chord alternate while the chord remains the same. The chord tones sound on the "and" of the beat, or in between the beats; the bass notes occur on the down beats.

EL RANCHO GRANDE
Duet

Ascending and Descending Slurs: Ligados

The purpose of this exercise is to strengthen the left hand ascending and descending slurs so that they may be played with ease when encountered in music.

Track 120

Left-Hand Agility Exercise

The purpose of this exercise is to develop finger independence and agility in the left hand. The bass notes should be played with the thumb and the upper notes with the fingers.

Track 121

Chords in C Major and A minor

The following chords are found in the keys of C Major and A minor. The first chord is C Major and uses five strings. There are two versions (voicings) of the G Major chord. The first uses an open second string. The second uses the "D" on the second string. Both of the G Major chords use all six strings. The G7 chord uses the 7th note of the scale above "G" (in the key of C), which is the "F" on the first string. This chord has a root, third, fifth, and (flat) seventh. The F Major chord is a barré chord. The barré at the first fret is notated in the music by the symbol (CI). The "C" means *Cejilla* or "to barré" in Spanish. The first finger frets the 6th, 2nd and 1st strings. The A minor chord uses five strings and is the tonic (i) chord in the key of A minor. The E Major chord is shown in two voicings. The first uses four strings and the second uses six. The "G♯" comes from the A harmonic minor scale. The "G♯" makes the E triad major instead of minor. The E7 chord uses the seventh note in the scale above "E," which is "D." This chord has a root, third, fifth, and seventh. The E chord is the dominant (V) chord in A minor. The D minor chord uses four strings and is built on the fourth note of the A minor scale. It is the sub-dominant (IV) chord in A minor.

Track 122

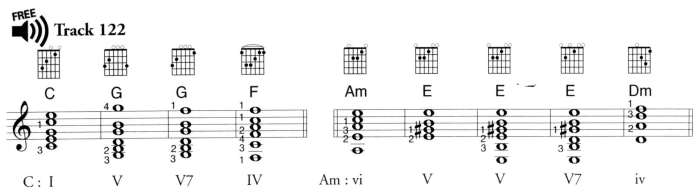

107

Las Mañanitas

"Las Mañanitas" is a popular Mexican folk song that is played for special occasions. Here it serves as a study in chord/melody playing.

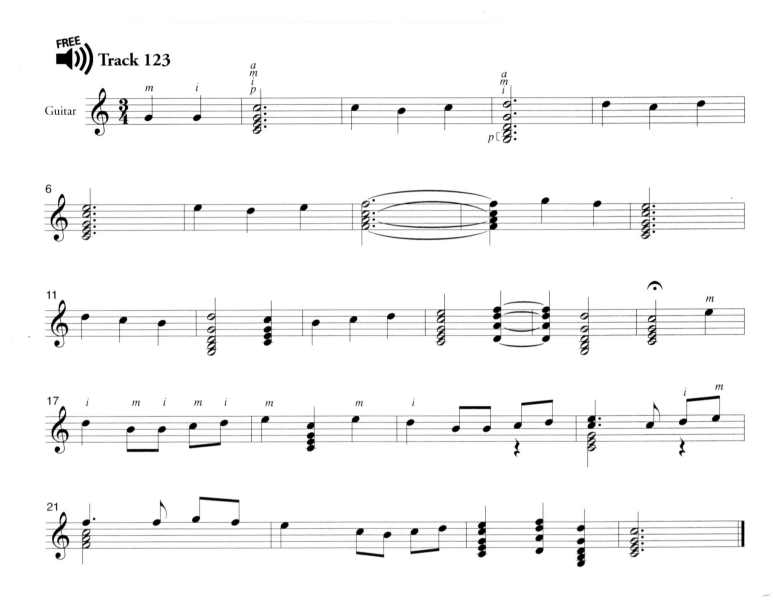

Greensleeves

The small notes that appear in the second measure of the fourth line on the first beat are called **grace notes**. The first grace note (G♯) is played on the beat with the open E bass note. Then hammer the 2nd finger onto the second fret and pull-off back to the first. This motion should be done as quickly as possible. At the end of the 4th line of music the notes C, E and G appear in the fifth position, or at the fifth fret. They may be played with the first finger barré or with fingers 2, 3, and 4. The C is on the fifth fret of the 3rd string. The E is at the fifth fret of the 2nd string. "Greensleeves" is a study in alternating between playing chords, note pairs, single notes, and grace notes.

GREENSLEEVES

SCALES AND CHORD PROGRESSIONS

C Major Scale (2 Octaves)

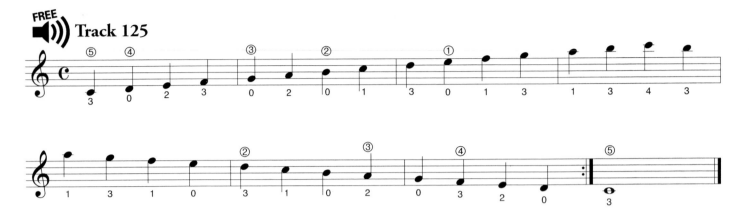

I-V-I-IV-I-VI Progression in C Major

The symbol CI indicates a barré, or partial barré, at the 1st fret. In this case, the first finger presses the first and second strings in measure seven.

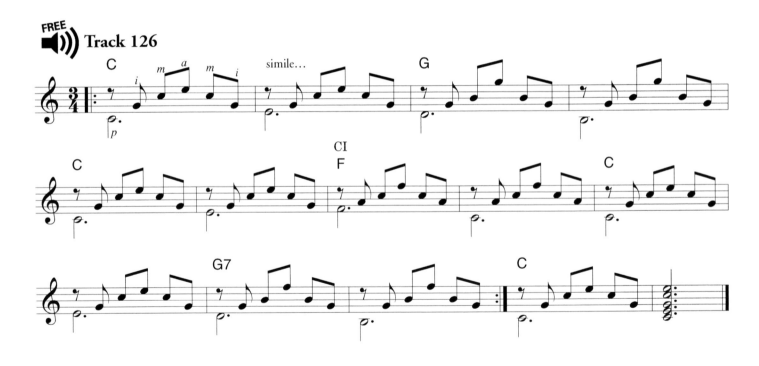

The progressions for C, G, D, A and their relative minor keys are shown below each scale. The rest of the principal chords can be found at the end of the scale section. Try the other right-hand arpeggio patterns with these progressions as well as rasgueado patterns shown in the beginning of the book. Each of the following scales and chord progressions are played twice on the recording. A repeat sign has been included at the beginning of each example as a reminder to repeat each exercise oneself until both hands feel synchronized by pressing with the left hand and almost simultaneously striking the string with the right hand.

Triads in C Major

Track 127

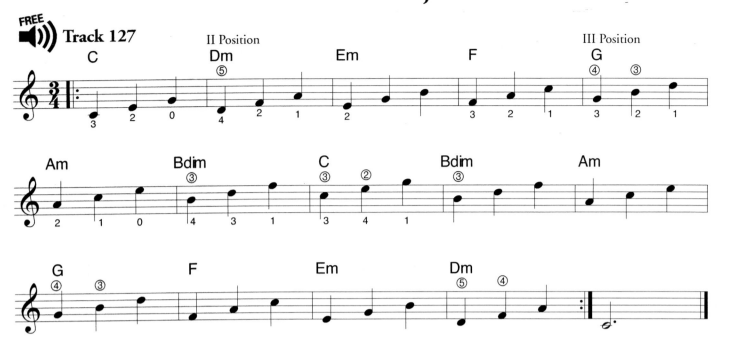

Rumba Rhythm

Here is a new rasgueado pattern that is a rumba flamenca rhythm. Apply it to the chord progression in 4/4.

Track 128

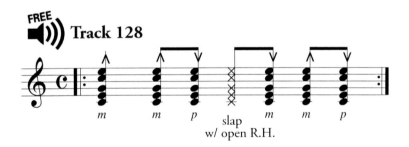

A Natural Minor Scale (2 Octaves)

Track 129

A Harmonic Minor Scale (2 Octaves)

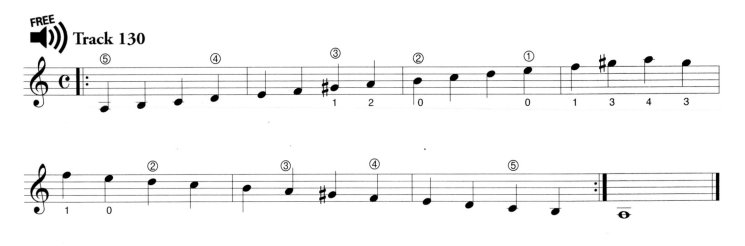

i-V-i-iv-i-V-i Progression in A Minor

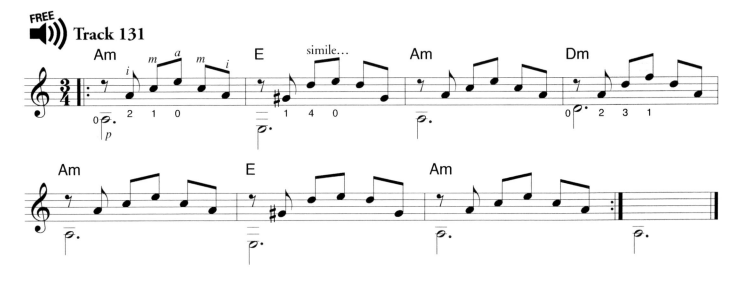

A Melodic Minor Scale (2 Octaves)

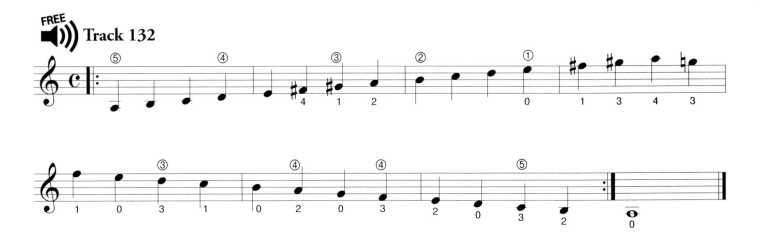

Transposition

In music, the term "transposition" means to move a note or a group of notes to a different pitch level. A major scale for example, may be played from any of the twelve musical pitches. The transposed scale must have the same arrangement of whole and half steps as the original, but will start on a different note than the original. In the G Major scale it is necessary to add the F-sharp in order to have the same arrangement of half steps and whole steps as the C Major Scale.

The first transposition example shows the C Major Scale transposed up a perfect fifth to "G." The transposed scale becomes G Major.

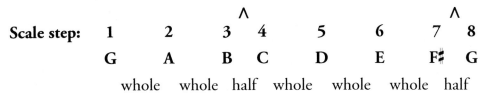

Scale step:	1	2	3	4	5	6	7	8
	G	A	B	C	D	E	F♯	G
	whole	whole	half	whole	whole	whole	half	

The G Major Scale

Track 133

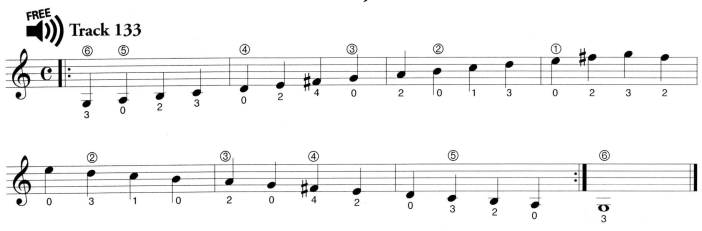

Triads in G Major

Track 134

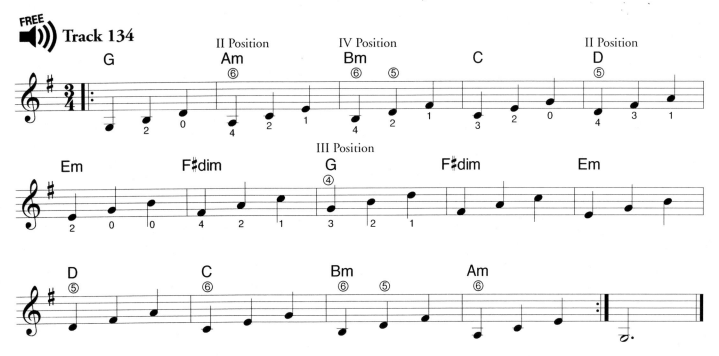

I-V-I-IV-I-V-I Progression in G Major

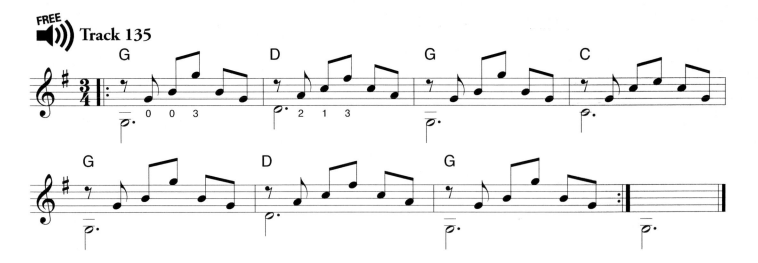

The F Major Scale

In the F Major scale, in order to keep the same arrangement of whole and half steps as in the C Major Scale, it is necessary to add the B-flat. All major scales have the same structure. The half steps must fall between scale steps 3-4 and 7-8. All other adjacent scale steps are whole steps.

Scale step:	1	2	3	^	4	5	6	7	^	8
	F	G	A		B♭	C	D	E		F
	whole	whole	half		whole	whole	whole	half		

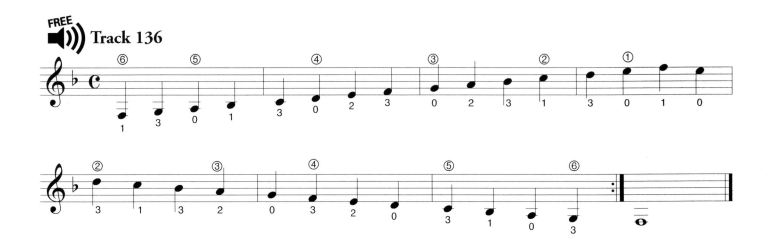

114

THE HOUSE OF THE RISING SUN

The purpose of learning this exerpt from "House of the Rising Sun" is to learn how an arpeggio pattern can be applied to a chord progression in popular music.

Traditional

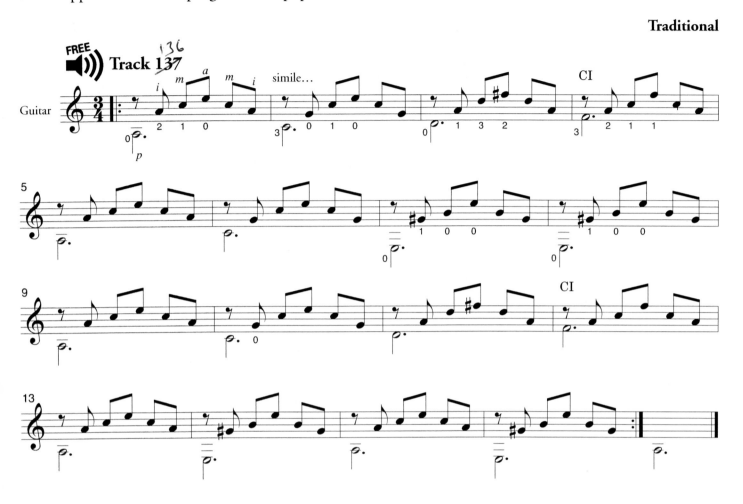

Variations on a Theme from Asturias

The theme in the bass part is from "Asturias (Leyenda)" by Isaac Albéniz. *Leyenda* means "legend." Asturias is a northern province in Spain as Seville and Córdoba are regions in the south. The regions in Spain are like the states in the United States.

The eighth notes with the small number 3 above the beam are **triplets**. This symbol means that the beat is divided into three equal parts, and there are three eighth notes per beat instead of two. The speed of the beat does not change. The eighth-note triplets are slightly faster than the regular eighth notes. The tremolo technique of repeated sixteenth notes is used on the first string in one variation. This figure is played *p, a, m, i*. These variations offer a study in playing arpeggio patterns while playing melody in the bass.

VARIATIONS ON A THEME FROM ASTURIAS

MALAGUEÑA

This arrangement is a combination of the flamenco and regional versions of "Malagueña." There are triplets in this composition in later variations. They should be played the same way as described in the introduction to "Variations on a Theme from Asturias." The rasgueado in the first line should be played with (down, up, down) strokes of the index finger until the sixteenth notes appear. At this point the (*i, s, a, m, i*) rasgueado is used twice in a row. The F Major chord in measure three has open first and second strings. The chord is commonly played this way and is easier to play than the full barré chord.

119

INTERVALS

In music, the term **interval** refers to the distance (the number of alphabetical letters) between two notes.

| Unison | Second | Third | Fourth | Fifth | Sixth | Seventh | Octave |

Each interval above is shown as a simultaneous **harmony** (two notes sounding together). The notes may sound at the same time or consecutively, but the interval is still the same.

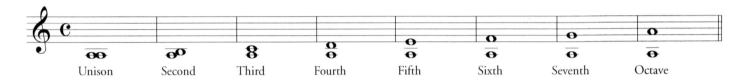

| Unison | Second | Third | Fourth | Fifth | Sixth | Seventh | Octave |

Interval Quality (Major, Minor, Perfect)

The number of an interval refers to the number of notes of the scale separating two notes, but since the major and minor scales do not have the same construction, (the half steps and whole steps lie in different places) the size of the thirds, sixths, and sevenths differ. Therefore, each interval must be classified further. Unisons, fourths, fifths, and octaves are classified as **perfect**, **diminished**, (smaller or more narrow by a half step) or **augmented**, (larger or wider by a half step). Seconds, thirds, sixths, and sevenths are classified most often as **major** or **minor**, and less frequently as augmented or diminished.

Interval Quality in the Major Scale

| Perfect Unison | Major Second | Major Third | Perfect Fourth | Perfect Fifth | Major Sixth | Major Seventh | Perfect Octave |

The major scale has a **perfect unison** (the same alphabetical letters that are zero half steps apart), a **perfect fourth** (the interval between two notes that are four alphabetical letters apart and also five half steps apart), and a **perfect fifth**, (the interval between two notes that are five alphabetical letters apart and seven half steps apart).

The major scale also has a **major second** (the interval between two notes that are two alphabetical letters apart and also two half steps apart) a **major third** (the interval between two notes that are three alphabetical letters and four half steps apart), a **major sixth** (the interval between two notes that are six alphabetical letters and nine half steps apart), and a **major seventh** (the interval between two notes that are seven alphabetical letters and eleven half steps apart). The last interval is the **perfect octave** (the interval between two notes that are eight alphabetical letters and twelve half steps apart).

Interval Quality in the Minor Scale

The minor scale has a **perfect unison** (the same alphabetical letters that are zero half steps apart), a **perfect fourth** (the interval between two notes that are four alphabetical letters and five half steps apart), and a **perfect fifth** (the interval between two notes that are five alphabetical letters and seven half steps apart).

The minor scale also has a **major second** (the interval between two notes that are two alphabetical letters and two half steps apart) a **minor third** (the interval between two notes that are three alphabetical letters and three half steps apart), a **minor sixth** (the interval between two notes that are six alphabetical letters and eight half steps apart), and a **minor seventh** (the interval between two notes that are seven alphabetical letters and ten half steps apart). The last interval is the **perfect octave** (the interval between two notes that are eight alphabetical letters and twelve half steps apart).

Interval Quality in the Harmonic Minor Scale

The harmonic minor scale has one different interval above the root note than the natural minor scale, the major seventh. There is also another more peculiar interval within the scale. The interval of the **augmented second** occurs between the sixth and seventh scale steps (see the last measure above).

Interval Quality in the Melodic Minor Scale

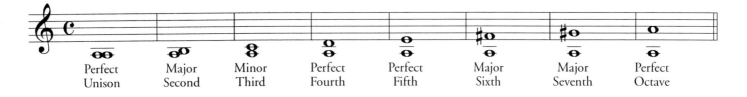

The melodic minor scale contains a major sixth and a major seventh.

CHORDS

A **chord** is defined as three or more notes sounding simultaneously. There are various kinds of chords:

Tertian — Based upon consecutive intervals of a third, for example C-E-G.
Clusters — Based upon consecutive seconds: e.g. E-F-G-G♯.
Quartal — Based upon consecutive fourths: e.g. A-D-G-C.
Quintal — Based upon consecutive fifths: e.g. A-E-B-F#.

Triads

Triads are a type of chord constructed by playing any note of the scale such as "A" and then adding the third and the fifth scale degrees above that note. Strictly speaking, a triad is a chord consisting of three notes that are separated by the interval of a third (three alphabetical letters apart). A triad based upon the note "A" in the key of C major or A minor is spelled: A-C-E.

A B **C** D **E** F G A

The note "A" is called the **root** because it is the note upon which the chord is based.

The note "C" is called the **third** because it is the third scale degree higher than "A." The "A" is counted as the first note; "B" is the second note above "A," and so on.

The note "E" is called the **fifth** because it is the fifth scale degree above the "A."

The interval from the note "A" to "C" is a minor third. The interval from the note "A" to "E" is a perfect fifth. The triad or chord quality is minor.

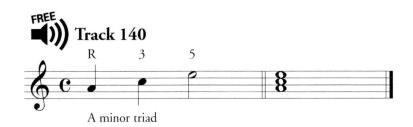

Track 140

A minor triad

The C Major Triad — I

In the C major scale, a triad based upon the note "C" is spelled C-E-G. The interval from "C" to "E" is a major third. The interval from "C" to "G" is a perfect fifth. The chord quality is major. The C major triad built upon the first note of the C major scale is called the tonic chord when referring to its function within the group of chords that may be built from the notes of the C major scale. The triad built upon the first note of any major or minor scale is called the **tonic**. The tonic is also referred to numerically with the Roman numeral I. The Roman numeral I indicates that the chord is built upon the first note (tonic, root) of the major scale and that its quality is major.

Track 141

C major triad

The C Major Arpeggio and Chord Inversion

Any note of the C major chord may serve as the lowest sounding note. When the note "C" (the root of the C major chord) is the lowest note, the chord is in **root position**. When the note "E" (the third of the C major chord) is the lowest note, the chord is in **first inversion**. When the note "G" (the fifth of the C major chord) is the lowest note, the chord is in **second inversion** as shown in the last measure of Ex. 143.

FREE  Track 143

The A Minor Triad — vi

In the C major scale, the triad based upon the note "A" is spelled A-C-E. The interval from "A" to "C" is a minor third. The interval from "A" to "E" is a perfect fifth. The chord quality is minor. The A minor triad is built upon the sixth degree of the C major scale and is called the sub-mediant when referring to its function within the group of chords that may be built from the notes of the C major Scale. The triad built upon the sixth degree of any major scale is called the **sub-mediant**. The sub-mediant is also referred to numerically with the Roman numeral vi. The Roman numeral vi indicates that the chord is built upon the sixth note of the scale; the lower case indicates that its quality is minor.

A minor triad

The A Minor Arpeggio and Chord

FREE  Track 145

123

The G Major Triad — V

In the C major scale, a triad based upon the note "G" is spelled: G-B-D. The interval from "G" to "B" is a major third. The interval from "G" to "D" is a perfect fifth. The chord quality is major. The G major triad is built upon the fifth note of the C major scale and is called the dominant when referring to its function within the group of chords that may be built from the notes of the C major scale. The triad built upon the fifth note of any major scale is called the **dominant**. The dominant is also referred to numerically with the Roman numeral V. The upper-case Roman numeral V indicates that the chord is built upon the fifth degree of the scale and that its quality is major.

A triad based upon the note "G" in the key of C is spelled G-B-D.

The G Major Arpeggio and Chord

The G Major chord at the end of Ex. 147 is in root position and has no fifth (D). While the chord is incomplete, it still functions as G major and sounds almost the same.

The F Major Triad — IV

In the C major scale, a triad based upon the note "F" is spelled F-A-C. The interval from "F" to "A" is a major third. The interval from "F" to "C" is a perfect fifth. The chord quality is major. The F major triad is built upon the fourth degree of the C major scale and is called the **sub-dominant** when referring to its function within the **key** (see p.141).

The sub-dominant is also referred to numerically with the upper-case Roman numeral IV; indicating that the chord is built upon the fourth degree of the scale (sub-dominant) by use of the Roman numeral IV; its quality is major as indicated by the use of the upper case.

Barré Chords

The F Major Arpeggio and Chord

The F Major chord at the end of the following example is is said to be in "first inversion" because the third of the chord "A" is the lowest note. The 1st finger of the left hand should simultaneously press the 1st and 2nd strings at the 1st fret. This technique is called a **barré**. Such chords are referred to as **barré chords** (also "barré" and "bar" chords).

F major triad

CHORD PROGRESSIONS

A **chord progression** is the movement from one chord to another and may include any number of chords. At least two chords are required to create a chord progression. Exercises 149-158 use the tonic, sub-dominant and dominant chords in the key of C Major and apply previously learned right-hand arpeggio patterns to the progression. Repeat each example as many times as necessary. Practice with a metronome and try not to slow down the tempo as the chords change.

126

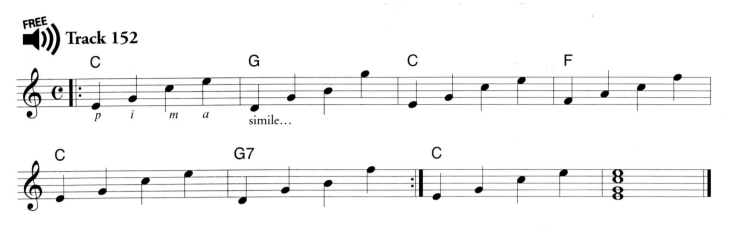

Track 152

Track 153

Track 154 153

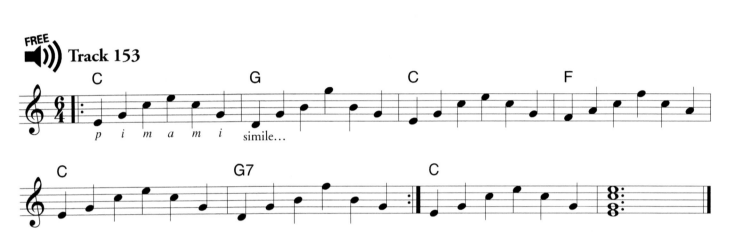

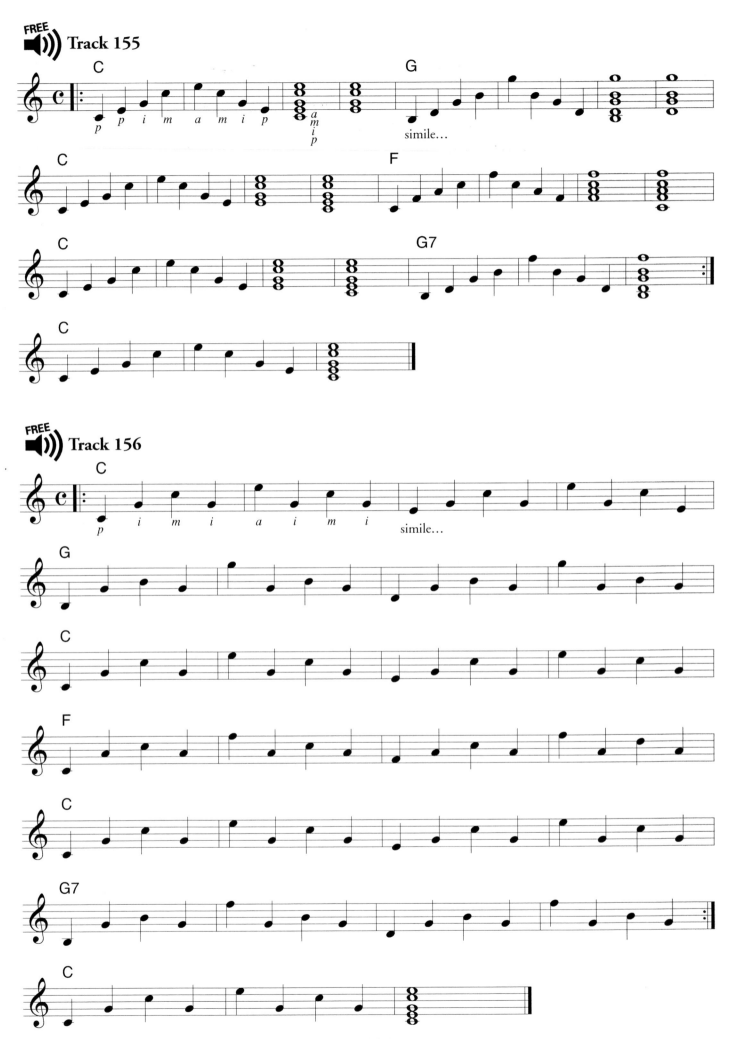

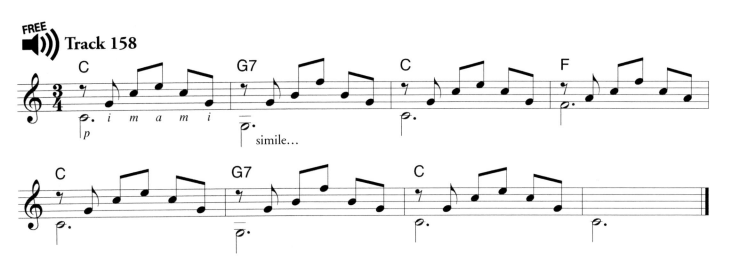

PETENERA

The following two compositions are studies in the alternation between 6/8 and 3/4 time. The first measure is in 6/8 time and the second is in 3/4. This alternation between 6/8 and 3/4 continues for the duration of Petenera with the exception of mm. 16-18 being in 3/4. The alternation of 6/8 and 3/4 resumes in m. 19.

Tales of the mysterious deaths of the performers of the Petenera have contributed to the "black legend" (*leyenda negra*) associated with it, causing some to refrain from uttering its name.

CAFÉ DE CHINITAS
(Petenera)

Federíco García Lorca

Guitar

LA VIRGEN DE LA MACARENA

"La Virgen de la Macarena" is a popular Spanish song. This arrangement offers a study in playing melody, bass and chords. The chords may be played with the index finger or thumb. Play downstrokes on the downbeats and upstrokes on the upbeats when playing the chords. Quickly move the thumb or index finger across the strings so that the attack of all six strings is almost simultaneous.

The High D and E on the First String

D – 10th fret   E – 12th fret

PICA-PICA MELODY
(Guitar I)

Track 162

Play 3x, then D.C. al Fine   *Fine*

PICA-PICA ACCOMPANIMENT
(Guitar II)

"Pica-Pica" is a Venezuelan waltz in A minor. The accompaniment pattern is generally characterized as a bass note followed by the fingers striking chords on beats two and three. Often referred to in slang as a "boom-chick-chick" accompaniment pattern, it can be applied to any chord progression.

PICA-PICA ACCOMPANIMENT
(Guitar III)

PICA-PICA ACCOMPANIMENT
(Guitar IV)

Track 165

PICA-PICA (QUARTET)

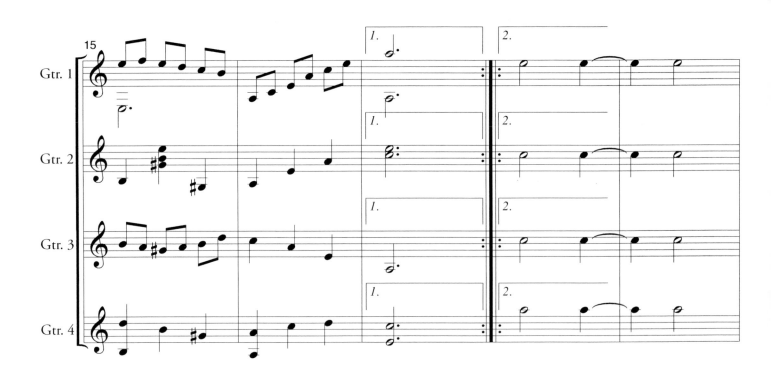

KEY

The term **key** refers to the heirarchical relationships between the notes of a **scale**, a stepwise progression of notes, e.g., C D E F G A B C, and their associated set of **triads**. The first note of the scale is called the **root**, which is also referred to as the **tonal center**.

So far, we have examined four chords that are all built from the notes of the C major scale. These chords are all closely related to one another because they are in the same key, C major. They have a hierarchical relationship to one another with each chord having a different level of importance.

The **tonic (I)** chord, C major (spelled C-E-G), is the most important chord because a piece of music usually begins and ends with the tonic chord. The second most important chord is the **dominant (V)** chord G major (spelled G-B-D), because it is the chord that leads back to the tonic. It is based on the fifth note of the scale, G. Nearly equal in rank to the dominant chord is the B **diminished, leading tone (vii°)** chord (spelled B-D-F). This is based on the seventh note of the scale and has two notes in common with the dominant chord. The chord that leads away from the tonic and toward the dominant is the **sub-dominant (IV)** chord F major (spelled F-A-C); this is the next most important chord in the key of C major. It is based on the fourth note of the scale. The **supertonic (ii)** chord, D minor, (spelled D-F-A) has two notes in common with the sub-dominant chord. It is based upon the second note of the scale. The supertonic chord serves the same purpose as the sub-dominant chord. It leads away from the tonic toward the dominant. The **sub-mediant (vi)**, A minor, is based upon the 6th note of the scale and is spelled A-C-E. It ranks equally with the **mediant (iii)** chord, E minor, based on the third note of the scale (spelled E-G-B). Both chords have at least two notes incommon with the tonic (I) chord.

CHORD SUBSTITUTION

In the key of C major, the **sub-mediant vi** chord (A-C-E) is a substitute for the **tonic chord I** (C-E-G) and may be used in its place because it shares two of three notes with the tonic chord, C and E.

The **supertonic ii** chord (D-F-A) is a substitute for the **sub-dominant IV** chord because they share two of three notes, F and A.

The **mediant iii** chord (E-G-B) is a substitute for either the **tonic I** chord (C-E-G) or the **dominant V** chord (G-B-D) because it shares two notes with each.

The **supertonic ii** chord, **mediant iii** chord, and **leading tone vii°** chord will be covered in volume two of this book series. It is important to first learn to play the primary chords in each key: I, IV and V.

KEY SIGNATURES

A key signature is a collection of sharps or flats placed at the beginning of a musical composition or section thereof. The key signature affects specific notes for the entire musical composition unless they are cancelled by a natural (♮) or another key signature change. The key signatures of C major and A minor contain no sharps or flats.

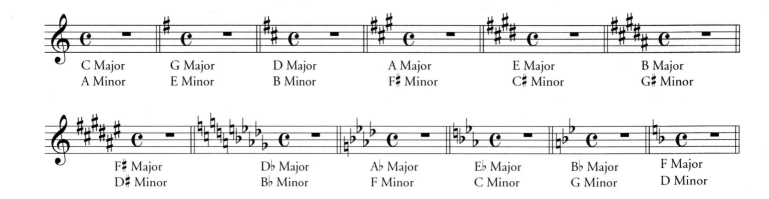

| C Major | G Major | D Major | A Major | E Major | B Major |
| A Minor | E Minor | B Minor | F♯ Minor | C♯ Minor | G♯ Minor |

| F♯ Major | D♭ Major | A♭ Major | E♭ Major | B♭ Major | F Major |
| D♯ Minor | B♭ Minor | F Minor | C Minor | G Minor | D Minor |

THE CIRCLE OF FIFTHS

The major keys are noted in capital letters and the minor keys in lower case letters. The number of sharps or flats required for each is shown inside each portion of the pie chart.

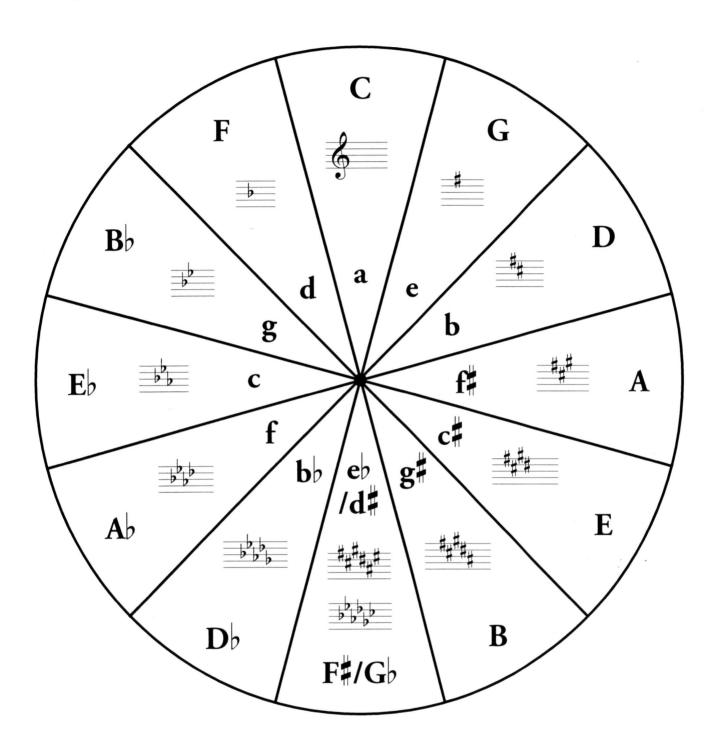

MAJOR AND MINOR SCALES IN THE FIRST POSITION
(in the Circle of Fifths)

C Major

I-V-I-IV-I-V-I Progression in C Major

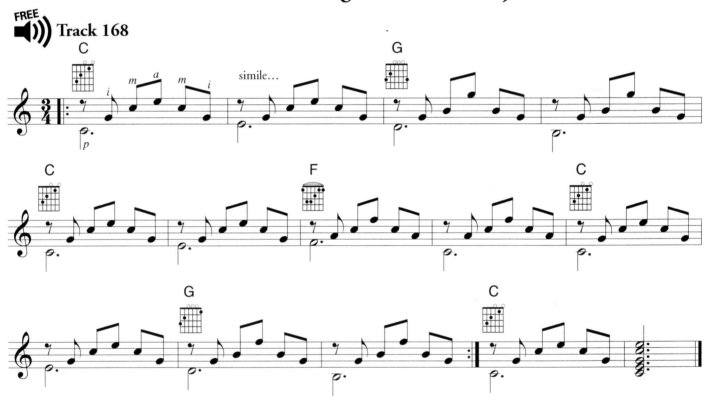

A Natural Minor

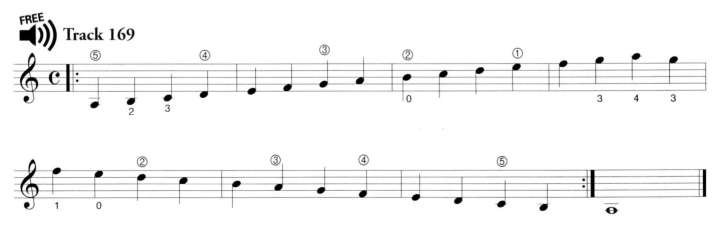

A Harmonic Minor

Track 170

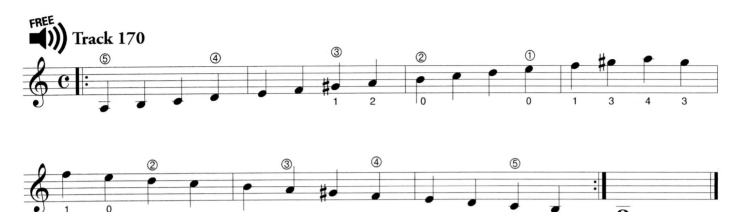

A Melodic Minor

Track 171

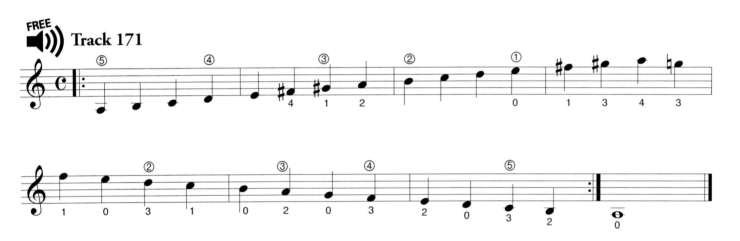

i-V-i-iv-i-V-i Progression in A minor

Track 172

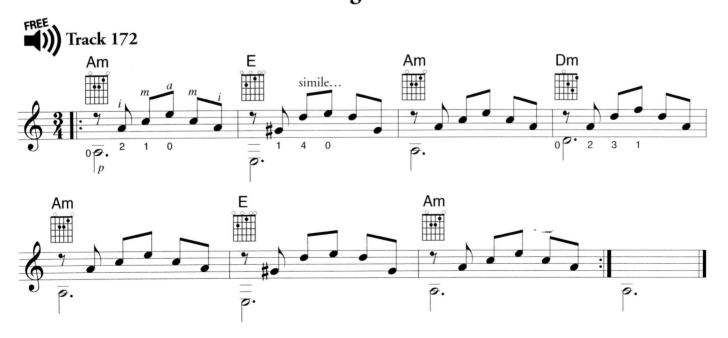

G Major

I-V-I-IV-I-V-I Progression in G Major

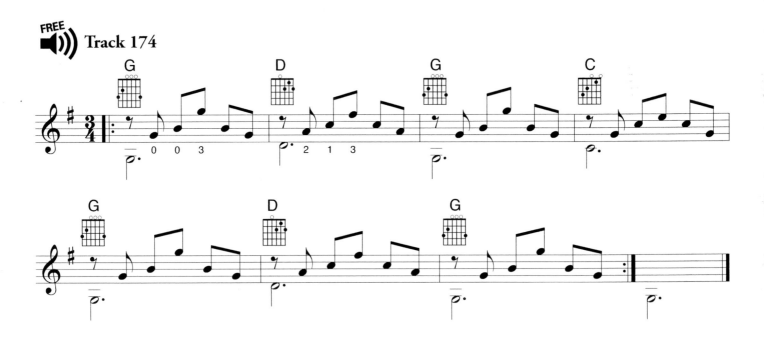

E Natural Minor

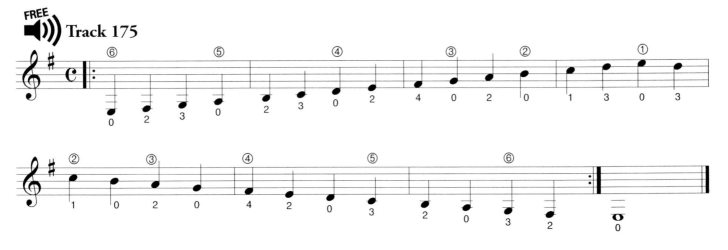

146

E Harmonic Minor

Track 176

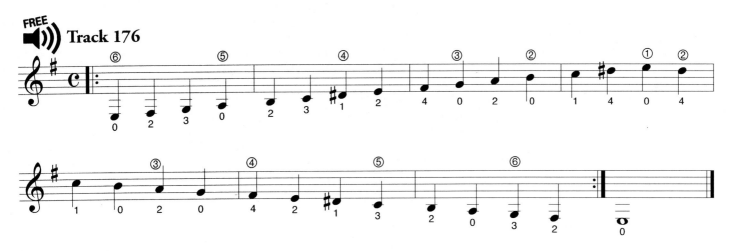

E Melodic Minor

Track 177

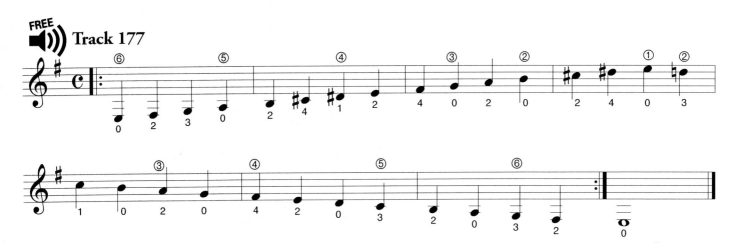

i-V-i-iv-i-V-i Progression in E Minor

Track 178

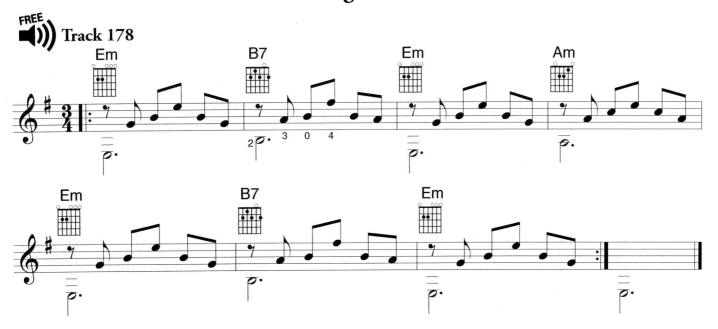

D Major

FREE Track 179

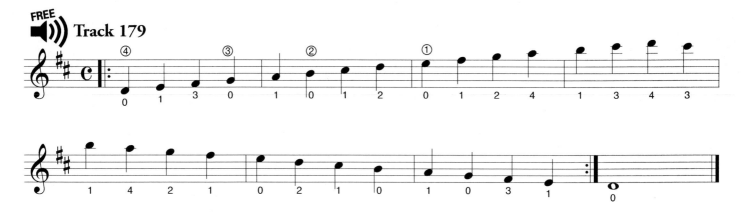

I-V-I-IV-I-V-I Progression in D Major

FREE Track 180

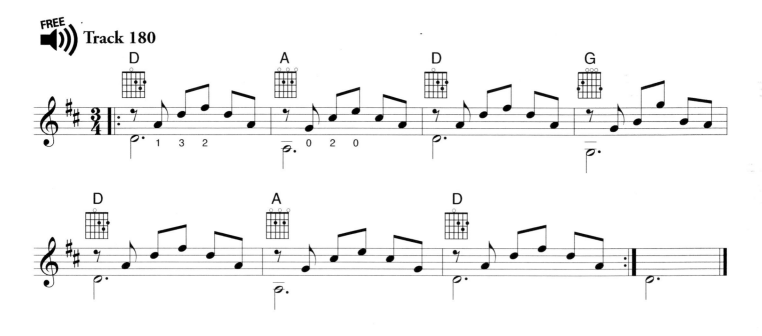

B Natural Minor

FREE Track 181

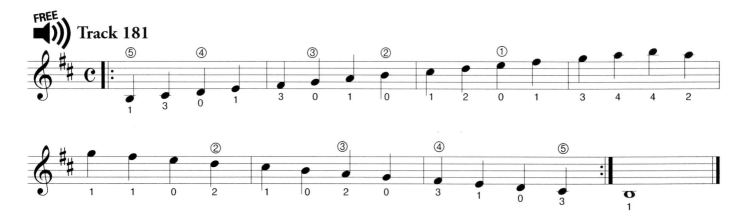

B Harmonic Minor

Track 182

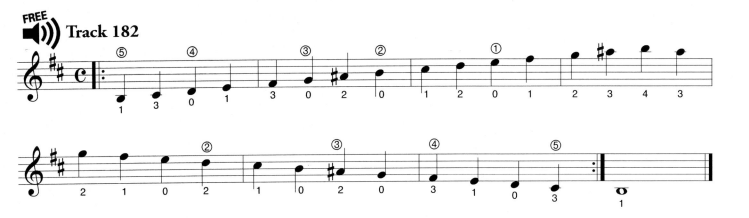

B Melodic Minor

Track 183

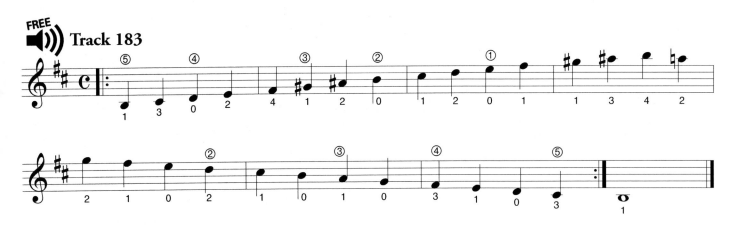

i-V-i-iv-i-V-i Progression in B Minor

Track 184

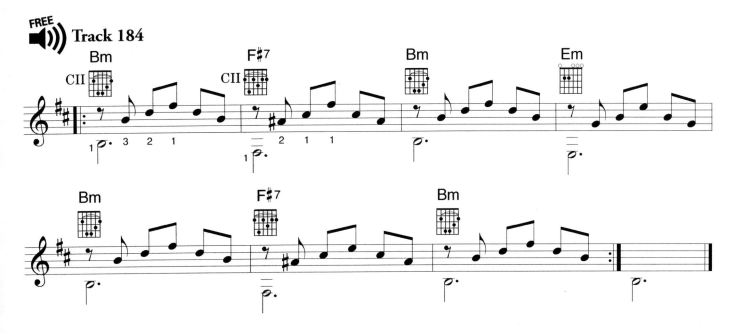

A Major

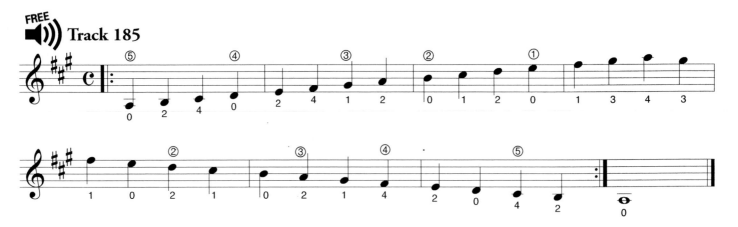

I-V-I-IV-I-V-I Progression in A Major

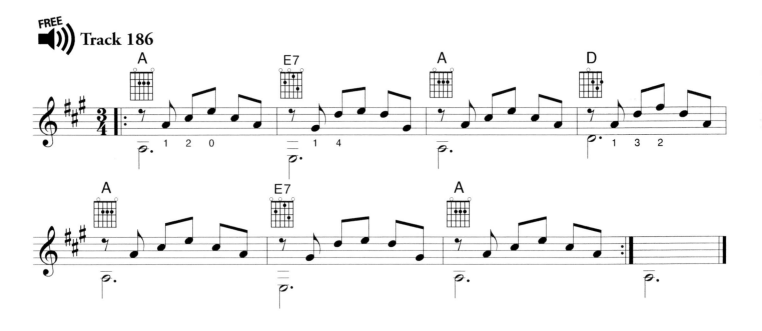

F♯ Natural Minor

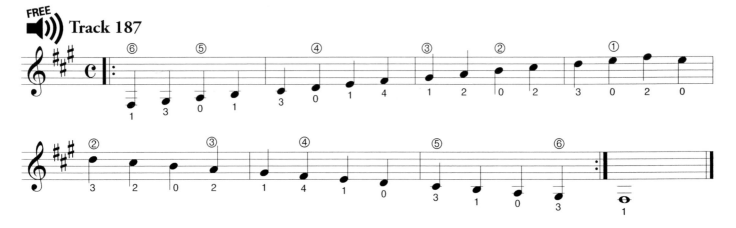

F♯ Harmonic Minor

FREE Track 188

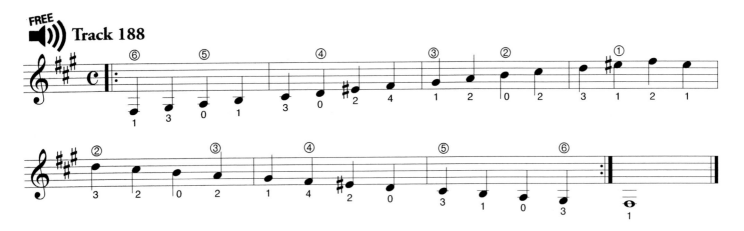

F♯ Melodic Minor

FREE Track 189

i-V-i-iv-i-V-i Progression in F♯ Minor

FREE Track 190

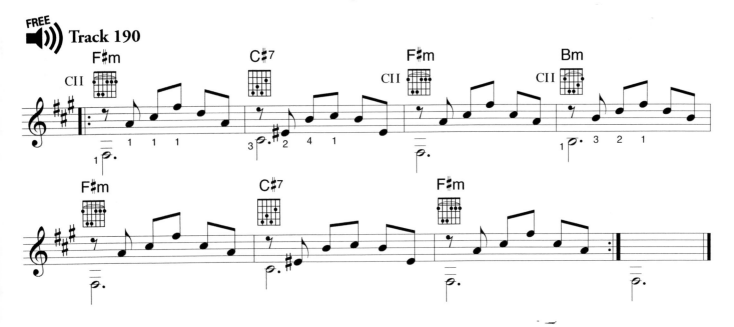

All chords for progressions in the following keys may be found in the chart on p.160.

E Major

FREE Track 191

C♯ Natural Minor

FREE Track 192

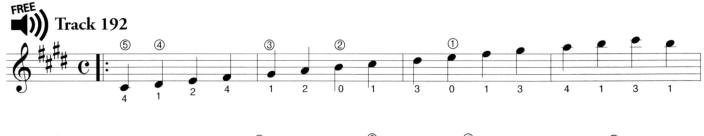

C♯ Harmonic Minor

FREE Track 193

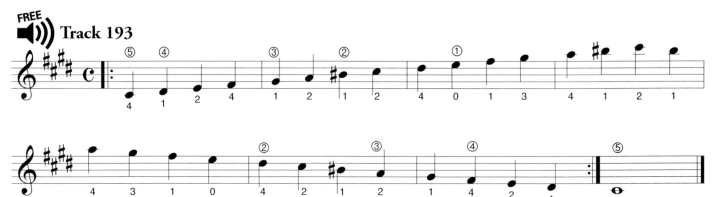

C♯ Melodic Minor

FREE Track 194

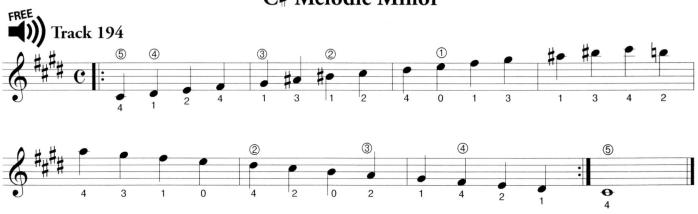

B Major

FREE Track 195

G♯ Natural Minor

FREE Track 196

G♯ Harmonic Minor

Since the "F♯" already exists in the G♯ pure minor scale, the raised 7th is F **double sharp**. The double sharp symbol (✗) looks like a boldface letter "x" and raises the note one additional half step. The **double flat** (♭♭) is not present here but is used in certain chords. It is not necessary to use the double flat in any scale in the circle of fifths. The double flat will be discussed in a later volume.

FREE Track 197

G♯ Melodic Minor

FREE Track 198

F♯ Major

FREE Track 199

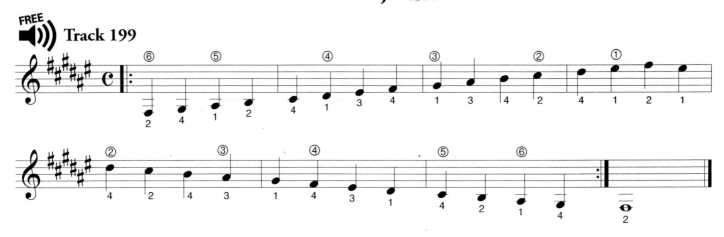

D♯ Natural Minor

FREE Track 200

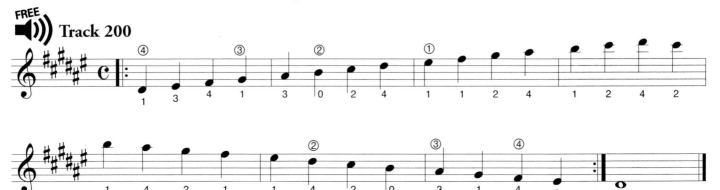

D♯ Harmonic Minor

FREE Track 201

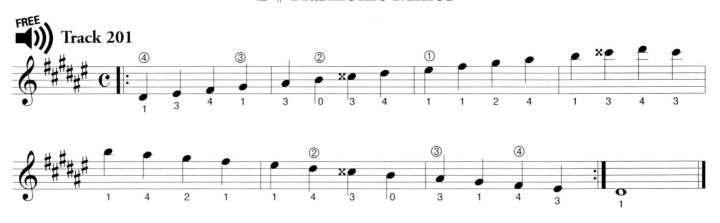

D♯ Melodic Minor

FREE Track 202

Db Major

Track 203

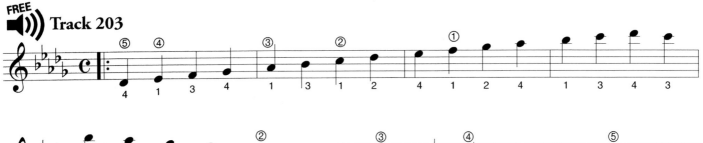

Bb Natural Minor

Track 204

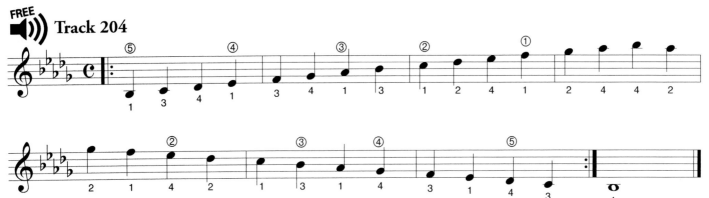

Bb Harmonic Minor

Track 205

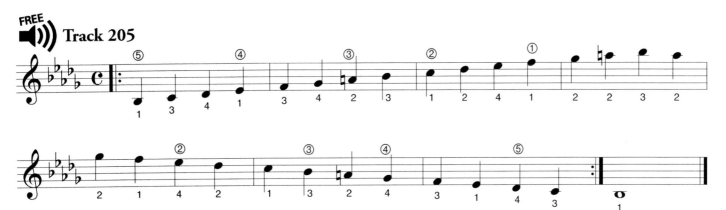

Bb Melodic Minor

Track 206

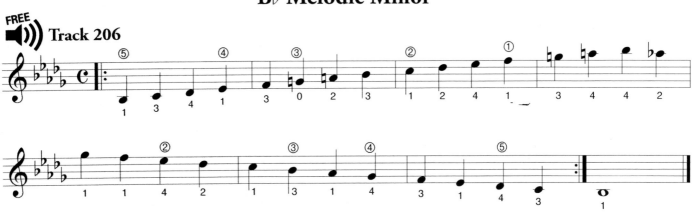

Ab Major

FREE Track 207

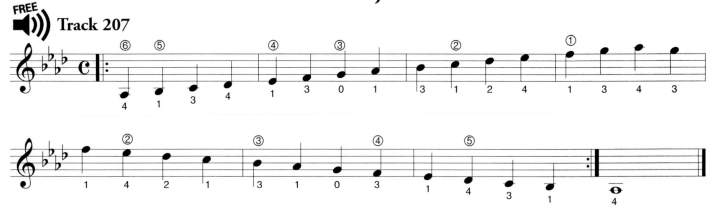

F Natural Minor

FREE Track 208

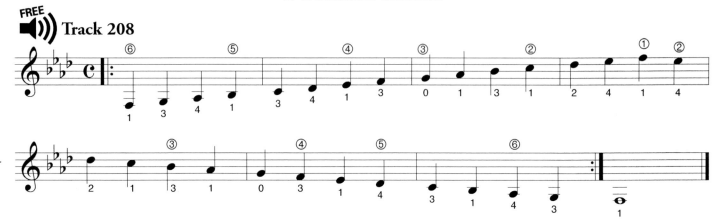

F Harmonic Minor

FREE Track 209

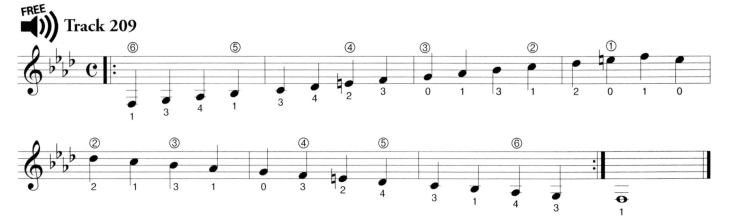

F Melodic Minor

FREE Track 210

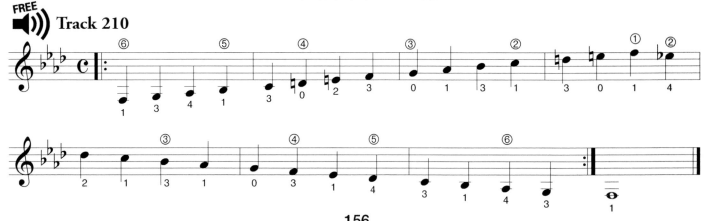

E♭ Major

FREE Track 211

C Natural Minor

FREE Track 212

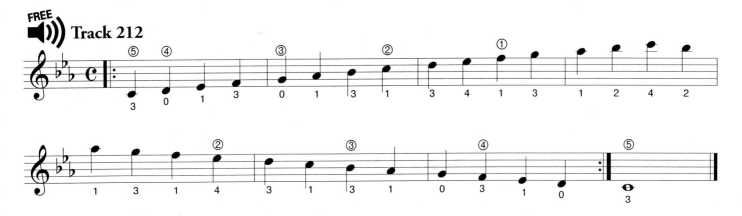

C Harmonic Minor

FREE Track 213

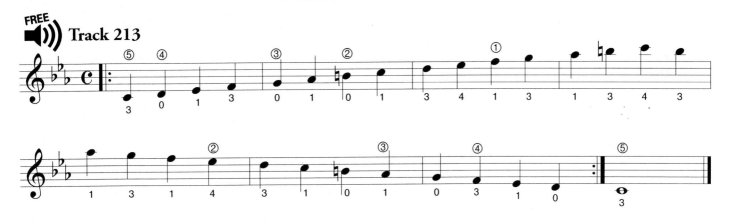

C Melodic Minor

FREE Track 214

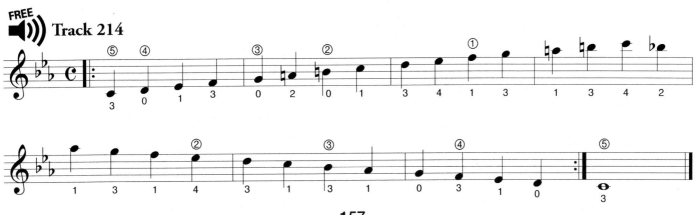

Bb Major

FREE Track 215

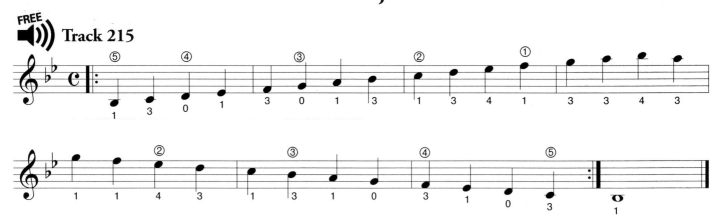

G Natural Minor

FREE Track 216

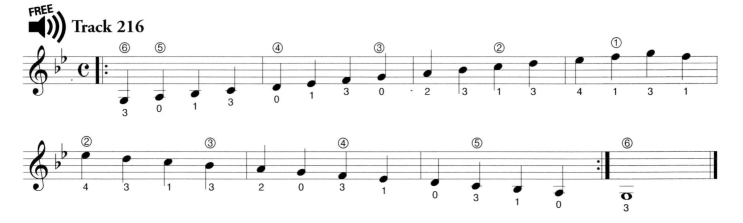

G Harmonic Minor

FREE Track 217

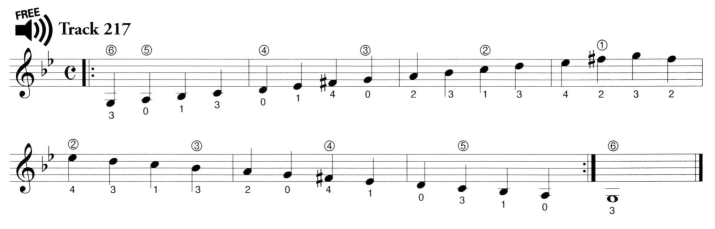

G Melodic Minor

FREE Track 218

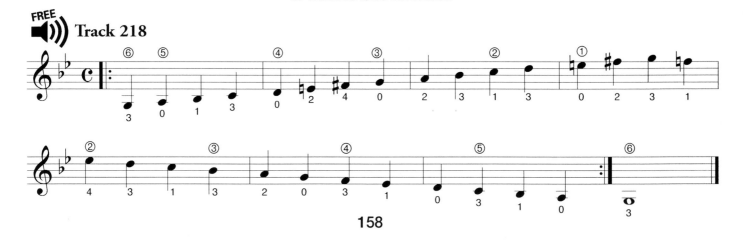

F Major

FREE Track 219

D Natural Minor

FREE Track 220

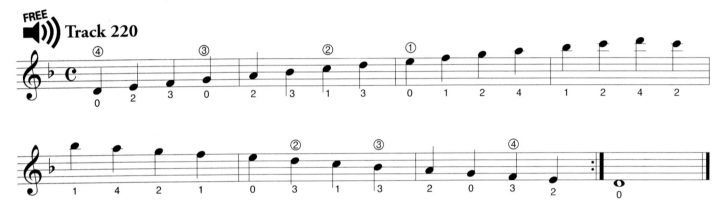

D Harmonic Minor

FREE Track 221

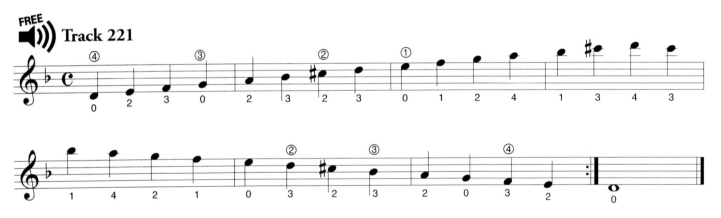

D Melodic Minor

FREE Track 222

MORE CHORDS IN THE CIRCLE OF FIFTHS

ALLEGRO

"Allegro" by Ferdinand Carulli (1770-1841) is a study in alternating the *p, i, m, a* argeggio with parallel tenths while playing rest stroke in the bass. The study is in the key of A minor.

Ferdinand Carulli

Track 223

ALLEGRETTO

"Allegretto" by Ferdinand Carulli (1770-1841) should be played with reststroke in the bass and freestroke in the upper part. This etude prepares the student for comfortably playing rest stroke basses in all contexts, alone or simultaneously with other notes. This composition is in the key of G major with the exception of mm. 17-24, which are in E minor.

Ferdinand Carulli

ANDANTE

"Andante" by Ferdinand Carulli (1770-1841) emphasizes parallel thirds and scales in the key of A minor in the "A" section. Make a smooth transition rhythmically from the scale passages to the parallel third passages. Play free strokes throughout.

The "B" section is in the key of C major. It emphasizes parallel tenths (third + octave) and a recurring "G" **pedal tone**. The piece features separate melody and bass parts. Play free strokes in the bass part and reststrokes in the melody part.

In general, exaggerate the dynamic markings so that the volume levels and crescendi are audible from a distance. Project the sound of the instrument by pushing inward toward the soundboard with the right-hand fingers. Follow the same procedure regarding the dynamics in your entire repertoire. The last measure of the last line of music contains the words "*Da Capo al Fine*." This indicates the return to the beginning and the-continuation to "*Fine*" at the end of the "A" section without repeats.

163

164

ALLEGRO IN E MINOR

"Allegro in E Minor" emphasizes the *a* and *m* fingers in the arpeggios to develop independence between the two fingers. The "B" section is in the key of G major. Observe the *Da Capo al Fine* indication. Use freestrokes throughout.

Ferdinand Carulli

ETUDE IN G MAJOR

"Etude in G Major" is similar to the "Andante" in that it has a pedal tone, but the melody cannot be consistently played with a reststroke without stopping an adjacent string in the process. Play freestrokes in the melody and bass parts.

Ferdinand Carulli

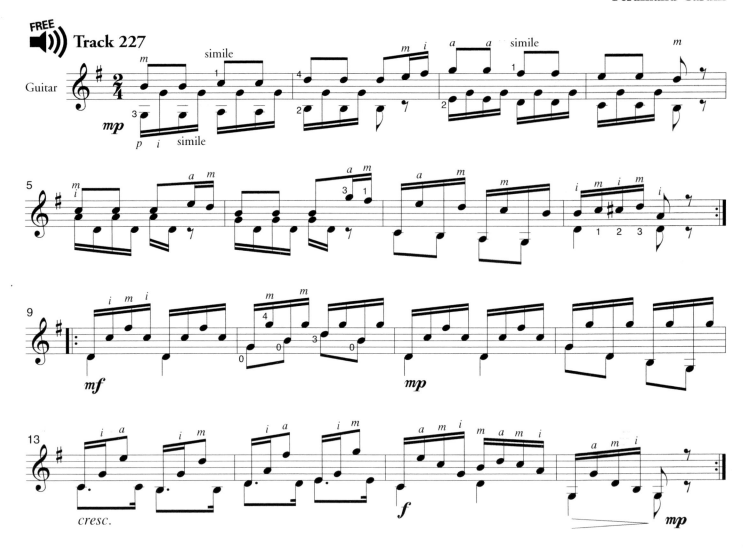

ANDANTINO

"Andantino" alternates between block chords and arpeggios. The purpose of this etude is to achieve balance between each voice in the block chords while maintaining good tone. It is easier to produce a good sound in playing the arpeggios. Try to match that sound in the block chord sections. At first, play the etude at least three times per practice session and emphasize each voice.

Ferdinand Carulli

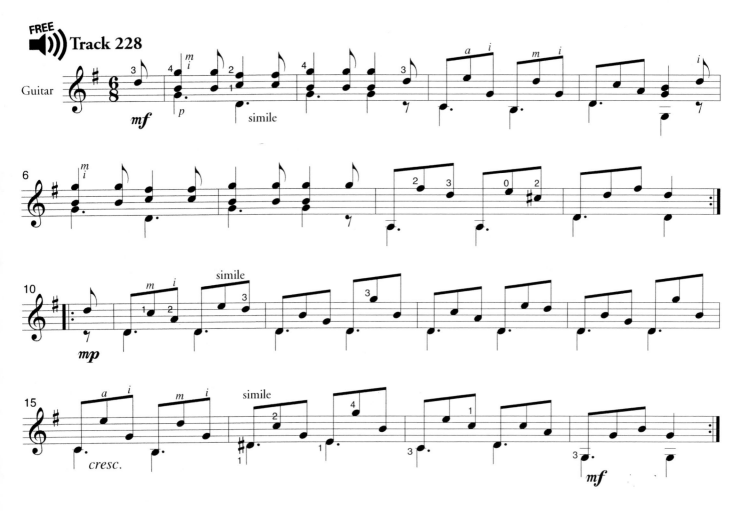

LARGHETTO

"Larghetto" is a study in parallel thirds while playing rest strokes in the bass. Play the melody using free strokes.

Ferdinand Carulli

ROMANZA

"Romanza" is slightly beyond the scope of this book because it makes use of the barré at the 5th, 7th and 9th positions. However, it is not too difficult and is quite gratifying to play, even if it requires a bit of hard work. Finger and string indications are given as usual but be sure to check the notes in the upper positions on the fingerboard chart if you are unsure about their locations.

Traditional

169

MENUET

"Menuet" by Robert de Visée (1650-1725) introduces the **trill**. In Baroque music, (ca.1600-1750) the trill is the rapid alternation of two notes. The trill may be executed on two different strings or on the same string. In this example, the latter is used. In m.1, the written melody note is C♯ and the trill begins on D. Press the 2nd finger on D and then rapidly pull-off to C♯, hammer-on to D and finally pull-off to C♯. This technique results in the sounding of four notes instead of one. Left-hand fingering suggestions are located next to each trill indication.

Robert de Visée

170

LECCIÓN 38

"Lección 38" by Dionisio Aguado (1784-1849) is in the key of E major and makes use of the half-barré ½CII. This technique requires that strings ①, ② and ③ be pressed simultaneously with the index finger.

Dionisio Aguado

CLARINES DE LOS MOSQUETEROS DEL REY DE FRANCIA

"Clarines de los mosqueteros del rey de Francia" by Gaspar Sanz (16??-1710) is from a *suite* or collection of short works that are played in succession without pause. The suite called "Clarins and trumpets with some very curious songs, both Spanish and from foreign nations" (1674) is in D major with the final movement in the parallel minor, D minor. In m. 3 there is a symbol above the F that indicates playing a **mordent**. Play the written note, quickly pull-off to E and then quickly hammer-on to F. The trill occurs for the first time in m. 5, beat 2. Many scholars agree that during this period in Spain the written note was played first, unlike the music of the rest of Europe, where the unwritten upper note was played first.

Gaspar Sanz

ALLEGRO

"Allegro" by Mauro Guiliani (1781-1829) requires consecutive preparation of the right-hand fingers in order to play at a fast tempo.

Mauro Guiliani

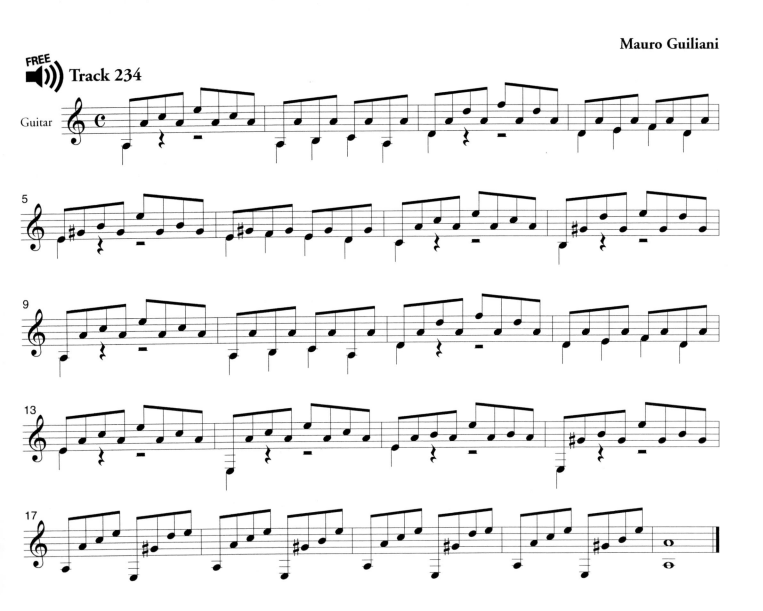

ANDANTE

"Andante" by Ferdinand Carulli (1770-1841) is in the key of F major. Using a pencil, mark your own fingerings where necessary.

Ferdinand Carulli

CONCLUSION

We hope that this book has helped you begin a continuing musical journey in performance of the great music in the flamenco/classical guitar repertoire. We have included selections that employ basic elements of music in a graded manner. There is much more to learn at this point about flamenco and classical guitar literature that you now have the tools to explore. Please refer to *Flamenco Guitar: Basic Techniques*, *The King of the Flamenco Guitar*, *The Falsetas of my Father: Antonio el del Lunar* and *Systematic Studies for Flamenco Guitar* by Juan Serrano. The next volume in this series contains more advanced techniques, repertoire in the higher positions, and much more.

ABOUT THE AUTHORS

Dr. Juan Serrano has been hailed by the San Francisco Chronicle as "The King of the Flamenco Guitar." His legendary career spans more than five decades as he was a child prodigy and international recording artist for Vik, Electra, and RCA Victor. He has performed in every cultural center in the world numerous times, has been involved in numerous film and television productions, and is a top-selling author of flamenco guitar method and repertoire books. His music and performances have inspired generations of guitarists around the world. He is currently a Distinguished Professor of Music at California State University, Fresno where he began the first Flamenco Guitar program in a university in 1983. He has been awarded the high honor of Honorary Doctor of Humane Arts and Letters from Fairfield University and holds a Master of Performance Degree from the Conservatory of Music in Córdoba, Spain. He gave the first-ever solo flamenco guitar performance in Spain (Córdoba 1960) and has accompanied every major flamenco singer and dancer in the world.

Dr. Corey Whitehead has performed in festivals and on television and radio in the United States, Brazil, Chile, Italy, France, Morocco, Jordan, Saudi Arabia, Kuwait, Bahrain, Yemen and China and has performed on numerous occasions at The John F. Kennedy Center for the Performing Arts, in Washington D.C. His duo "Douze Cordes" has performed in the Middle East, North Africa, and Chile on three tours as Cultural Ambassadors of the U.S. Department of State performing for royalty and dignitaries, in festivals, and on television and radio. He earned his Doctor of Musical Arts, Masters, and Bachelors Degrees in Guitar Performance at the University of Arizona under the tutelage of Thomas Patterson. He has studied extensively with Juan Serrano, at the Curso Flamenco XIV in Sanlúcar de Barremeda, Spain with Gerardo Núñez and in Córdoba, Spain in "La forma y naturaleza de la guitarra flamenca" with Manolo Sanlúcar. He is currently Professor in Flamenco and Classical Guitar Performance at California State University, Fresno and has previously taught at The Duke Ellington School of the Arts in Washington, D.C., The Levine School of Music in Washington, D.C., Northern Virginia Community College, Virginia Commonwealth University, and Pima Community College in Tucson, AZ.